D0327131

what do fist think of
soc. sci. research?

p150
└ lack of soc sc. research partially
suggests that the usual people who deal
w/ it are isolate issues from social web

p.157-8

p.2 view from social life = social sc
                        perspective
          └ is this fist view
               also in a way

— Wit. might also be upset by lack of soc. sc.
research b/ shows failure to think
ahead @ all implications

CHANGING HUMAN REPRODUCTION

CHANGING HUMAN REPRODUCTION

Social Science Perspectives

edited by

Meg Stacey

SAGE Publications
London · Newbury Park · New Delhi

Chapters 1, 2, 8 and editorial arrangement © Meg Stacey 1992
Chapter 3 © Naomi Pfeffer 1992
Chapter 4 © Sarah Franklin 1992
Chapter 5 © Frances Price 1992
Chapter 6 © Erica Haimes 1992
Chapter 7 © Marilyn Strathern 1992

First published 1992

All rights reserved. No part of this publication may
be reproduced, stored in a retrieval system,
transmitted or utilized in any form or by any means,
electronic, mechanical, photocopying, recording or
otherwise, without permission in writing from the
Publishers.

 SAGE Publications Ltd
6 Bonhill Street
London EC2A 4PU

SAGE Publications Inc
2455 Teller Road
Newbury Park, California 91320

SAGE Publications India Pvt Ltd
32, M-Block Market
Greater Kailash – I
New Delhi 110 048

British Library Cataloguing in Publication data

Changing Human Reproduction: Social
Science Perspectives
    I. Stacey, Meg
    306.461

    ISBN 0–8039–8653–X
    ISBN 0–8039–8654–8 (pbk)

Library of Congress catalog card number 92–056382

Typeset by The Word Shop, Bury, Lancashire.
Printed in Great Britain by Biddles Ltd, Guildford, Surrey.

Contents

Notes on Contributors

Sarah Franklin lectures in women's studies and cultural anthropology in the Department of Sociology at Lancaster University. She is the author of numerous articles on new reproductive technologies, co-editor of *Off-Centre: Feminism and Cultural Studies* (Routledge, 1991) and co-author of *Procreation: Kinship and the New Reproductive Technologies* (Manchester University Press, 1993).

Erica Haimes is a lecturer in the Department of Social Policy of the University of Newcastle. She gained her doctorate in 1990 for a thesis entitled 'Family Connections: the Management of Biological Origins in the New Reproductive Technologies' (University of Newcastle). Chapters and articles she has written and her continuing research interests cover the social implications of the new reproductive technologies, adoption, the family and the sociology of personal identity. She is co-author (with N. Timms) of *Adoption, Identity and Social Policy* (Gower, 1985).

Naomi Pfeffer writes about medical history, women's health, research ethics and social policy. Her publications include *The Experience of Infertility* (Virago, 1983), *Infertility Services: a Desperate Case* (Greater London Association of Community Health Councils, 1988) and chapters on 'The hidden pathology of the male reproductive system' (Gower, 1985) and 'Artificial insemination, in-vitro fertilization and the stigma of infertility' (Polity Press, 1989). She is completing *The Stork and the Syringe: a History of Medicine and Infertility in England in the Twentieth Century* (Polity Press, forthcoming).

Frances Price is a Senior Research Associate in the Child Care and Development Group in the Faculty of the Social and Political Sciences at the University of Cambridge. She is co-author of *Three, Four or More* (HMSO, 1990) and of *Procreation: Kinship and the New Reproductive Technologies* (Manchester University Press, 1993). Her recent publications include articles on the medical management of uncertainty, particularly in relation to assisted conception and obstetric ultrasonography; the dilemmas surrounding egg donation and selective reduction of multiple pregnancy; and the representation of science and technology in clinical practice.

Meg Stacey, Emeritus Professor of Sociology of Warwick University, has focused on issues in the sociology of health for the past 30 years, editing *Hospitals, Children and their Families* (Routledge and Kegan Paul, 1970) and (with David Hall) *Beyond Separation: Further Studies of Children in Hospital* (Routledge and Kegan Paul, 1979), and writing *The Sociology of Health and Healing* (Unwin Hyman, 1988). She served on the Welsh Hospital Board, the Michael Davies Committee on Hospital Complaints Procedure and, as a lay member, on the General Medical Council. From this derives *Regulating British Medicine: the General Medical Council* (Wiley, 1992).

Marilyn Strathern, Professor of Social Anthropology at Manchester University, has contributed to the anthropology of both Melanesia (with, for example, *Women in Between*, 1972; *The Gender of the Gift*, 1988) and Britain (*Kinship at the Core*, 1981; *After Nature*, 1992). Recently she has also compiled a collection of essays on anthropology, kinship and the new reproductive technologies: *Reproducing the Future* (Manchester University Press, 1992).

1

Introduction: what is the social science perspective?

This book presents a social science perspective on the issues surrounding the development and use of forms of new reproductive techniques, such as *in vitro* fertilization, semen and egg donation. The contents were first brought together in the Sociology Section of the 1990 Annual Meeting of the British Association for the Advancement of Science by the section president, Margaret Stacey, with the express purpose of demonstrating (i) that a distinctive social science perspective on these techniques exists; (ii) that problems arising from the use of these techniques, which might otherwise continue to trouble both users and providers, can be elucidated through the theoretical and empirical research carried out by social scientists; and (iii) that therefore such a perspective requires greater recognition.

The chapters cover a broad range of topics, from the history of infertility treatment, the responsibility for and consequences of multiple births, the notion of assisted kinship and the narratives surrounding the process of conception to the debate over the release of information about the identity of gamete donors. Each of these topics raises questions on a variety of levels: the conceptual (for example, can contemporary usages of the term 'kinship' embrace the developments in assisted reproduction when these developments appear to undermine the premises on which that term has previously been used?), the cultural (for example, what are the symbolic meanings attributed to the origins of persons in this society?), the political (for example, why in liberal democracies is involuntary childlessness seen as an issue of health and wellbeing and not a social or specifically a population problem?), and the practical (for example, how do parents cope with quads or quins?)

Other levels are also at issue, and this is the point. Investigations in this area require a critical awareness of the assumptions underlying the research, the complex and often contradictory dimensions of the issues being investigated, and the location of social science in relation to the knowledges, representations and practices about reproduction. These last are themselves transformed by the social science research concerning them and also transform the research.

What we wish to convey is the view from social life. Current technological advances in reproductive medicine affect people's lives, endorse certain values, run into stereotypes and have consequences for the management of relations that may extend well beyond their immediate application. They are in that sense part of society, and will help shape its future. To think of such technologies as having 'social' dimensions provides a way of thinking about the multiple nature of their impact. For if social life is a manifold and complex phenomenon, then the one perspective it affords is that of the complexity and interrelatedness of acts and effects. In terms of disciplines, that apprehension is by social science.

Since it is hoped that this collection will be read by a variety of professionals and by members of other disciplines, it is not enough merely to assert the benefits of a social science perspective. Rather, it is necessary to explicate further what we mean by that phrase and also to explore how such a perspective can become more widely recognized. That is what the rest of this introduction briefly sets out.

Among the social sciences, sociology predominates here. However, the crucial importance of history and anthropology for an understanding of the social has been argued by sociologists from Ginsberg to Giddens. As the latter argues:

> If the first dimension of the sociological imagination involves the development of an historical sensibility, the second entails the cultivation of anthropological insight. To say this is again to emphasize the tenuous nature of the conventionally recognized boundaries among the various social sciences. (1982: 22)

Although it is not the case in this collection that the two disciplines are seen as the servants of the third, we do find that the benefits of an interdisciplinary social science approach are numerous. Sociology provides the analysis of institutions within industrialized societies, such as the 'family', the 'state', 'law' and 'medicine', which underpin the technological interventions in reproduction, but which otherwise have a hidden or taken-for-granted character in discussions about clinical or social practice (Haimes, 1990: v). Through the concept of interest and its multiple modes of realization, sociology forces us to look at but also beyond the rhetoric used to justify the new techniques and consider whose needs and desires they serve: childless women and men, parents, children, professionals (medical or legal) or society in general? Anthropology provides the broader conceptual tools for the analysis of two recurrent themes in these discussions, that is, notions of kinship and relatedness and notions of what is 'natural'. Both these themes, explicitly or implicitly, run through many of the chapters. History reminds us not only of the perils of presuming the 'newness' of these issues but also makes us aware of the connections with past and future developments.

The links between the three disciplines represented here also mean that we provide a comparative perspective which ensures that our assumptions as social scientists as well as the assumptions of others are open to challenge and re-examination. This introduces another distinctive aspect of the social science approach, which has been identified by Giddens as the task of breaking free 'from the confines of the familiar' (1982: viii) and from thinking in terms only of the society in which we currently live (1982: 26). The task is made urgent by the very fact that the technologies being addressed here have *already altered* what can be taken for granted about reproductive processes (such as conception and pregnancy), reproductive identities (such as motherhood and parenthood) and reproductive ties and obligations (such as kinship). That such changes have mobilized considerable public concern is evident in the many debates surrounding them.

Many of the situations described in the following chapters appear to conflict with normal everyday expectations. It is commonly presumed that conceiving a baby is a straightforward matter, that most people will be genetically related to the parents who rear them, and that most women will have only one baby at a time. Such expectations encourage judgements and decisions which at best marginalize and at worst stigmatize those who apparently deviate from them. Questioning the status of those expectations can yield benefits by showing, from a comparative perspective, that they are arbitrary or ambiguous. Practically, the lives of specific individuals may directly be improved (for example, by feeling less stigmatized by their involuntary childlessness, by being given domestic and economic support to bring up children who have a disability or children from multiple births). Theoretically, the apparently normal is subjected to as much investigation and analysis as the apparently deviant and thus we learn more about what constitutes our ideas of 'society' and 'the social'.

This approach does necessarily lead to a critical stance, however, and one which can be uncomfortable for those working in the areas analysed. The approach has in the past also sometimes led social scientists to make inappropriate claims (cf. Moser, 1990). These claims have at one and the same time been too narrow and too extensive: too extensive in so far as they present the social scientist as the 'expert' on the 'social consequences' of these developments; too narrow when the social scientist is regarded merely as a 'social technician', to be called in once the parameters of the debate have been set by others. As the following chapters show, social scientists have as many questions to ask about the processes by which these 'issues' have been constructed and presented for public debate as they have about the 'issues' themselves.

This is not to assert a sense of the certainty of social science knowledge. That all knowledge is recognized as essentially contestable is a major benefit of comparative analysis. This opens up the possibility of a dialogue, enabling the contribution of social scientists to be recognized by other disciplines (Silverman, 1985). Dialogue comes from a recognition of the different ways each discipline constitutes its body of knowledge (in terms of its intellectual starting points, the kinds of questions being asked, its conceptual framework, theoretical assumptions, the methods of empirical investigation and analysis and finally what counts as an appropriate answer to the questions asked (see Cuff and Payne, 1984: 3). While no body of knowledge can make any absolutist claims, none the less each can claim to help us 'know better' (Cuff and Payne, 1984: 11) about hitherto unexplored areas.

Dialogue also makes explicit another feature which social sciences have in common with other disciplines: the commitment to sustained, systematic and rigorous inquiry. Such a commitment enables a series of connections to be made: connections between different branches of the social sciences and other disciplines; connections between apparently narrow aspects of applied reproductive techniques and broader questions about the nature of social order; connections between the theoretical, the empirical and the practical; connections between the past and present; and cross-cultural connections. Connections, it must be added, which are based on analysis, both theoretical and empirical, rather than mere opinion or prescription. These features characterize the chapters in this collection.

In Chapter 2 Meg Stacey discusses research in relation to developments in the medicalization of childbirth, particularly those associated with assisted reproduction. Starting from the assumption that birth is as much a social as a biological event, she finds the tardy involvement of the social sciences in these developments both disturbing and hard to understand. Naomi Pfeffer's historical account of the treatment for infertility which follows shows how, in order to evade the enactment of an overt population policy in Britain, this treatment was left, once serious medical attention was paid to it, largely to the private sector. She is disquieted by the failure to examine the organization of infertility services in the political round and by the absence of universality in the delivery of assisted reproduction.

Sarah Franklin then demonstrates in Chapter 4 how the way we think about and explain conception has been and is being crucially changed by the introduction of the new procedures. Drawing her data from interviews with mothers who have undergone IVE, most of them without achieving a live baby, she shows that our simple narrative about how babies are conceived is being complicated and elongated, now involving many more than two people. What was once seen as a simple natural process now appears as an obstacle race in which success is a miracle. In contrast to those who do not achieve a live baby, success for others means they give birth to three, four or more babies at once. Frances Price (Chapter 5) reports on the increased incidence of such multiple births following the introduction of medically assisted conception; she describes the meaning for the parents, and especially the mothers, of finding themselves with more children than they have breasts or hands. Her chapter draws particular attention to the lack of understanding about the help such mothers need and to the shortage of much needed support services.

The development and use of assisted reproduction is closely associated with the desire experienced by many in the Euro-American world to have a baby of 'their own'.

Paradoxically, techniques such as *in vitro* fertilization (IVF) and gamete intrafallopian transfer (GIFT) may mean that in practice the child who is born may lack biological connection to its social parents in a number of different ways – s/he may not have inherited genes from both her/his parents, or may not have been carried by the woman who is rearing her/him. This has given rise to many problems, one of which is whether the donors of eggs or semen should remain anonymous and in whose interest that might be. Erica Haimes in Chapter 6 describes the opposed opinions on this matter and reports on her interviews on the question with members of the Warnock Committee which inquired into the issue of human fertilization and embryology. Her analysis of the data shows that there is more common ground between the antagonists than one might expect, since the debate hinges around the importance attributed to biological origins in constituting the individual.

This theme is taken up by Marilyn Strathern in Chapter 7, where she discusses the implications of assisted reproduction for our cultural understanding of kinship: human kinship, she argues, is a fact of society rooted in facts of nature defining, in Euro-American society, who we are and who our 'real' relatives are. However, assisting reproduction changes the facts of nature, introducing uncertainty into this definition. In discussions of the resulting problems, such as those during the passing of the UK Human Fertilization and Embryology Act, 1990, a cultural asymmetry emerges: in talking about human beginnings no reference is made to social factors, whereas in the legal debate about who shall be *socially* acknowledged as parents constant reference is also made to *biological* parents. Recognizing this asymmetry is crucial in understanding how the medical interventions and the consequent legal decisions will change the kinship system and thus the way people think about each other.

In concluding the book we seek to show how, as social scientists, we have already been able to increase understanding of the meaning and implications of assisted reproduction. We also draw attention to the great need for further research into the relationships between the management of human reproduction and the reproduction of the culture and structure of our society.

By participating in the British Association for the Advancement of Science we have undertaken the task of communicating the contributions of our disciplines to other scientists and to the general public; by the range of substantive topics covered and the diversity of analyses offered, we demonstrate the breadth of the perspectives available to social science. By our commitment to the activities of social inquiry, namely asking questions and making connections, we also demonstrate the vitality of social science both as knowledge and as practice.

References

Cuff, E.C. and Payne, G.C.F. (eds) (1984) *Perspectives in Sociology,* 2nd edn. London: Allen and Unwin.

Giddens, A. (1982) *Sociology: a Brief but Critical Introduction.* London: Macmillan.

Haimes, E. (1990) 'Family Connections: the Management of Biological Origins in the New Reproductive Technologies'. Doctoral thesis, Department of Social Policy, University of Newcastle.

Moser, C. (1990) 'The need for an informed society'. Presidential address to the British Association for the Advancement of Science.

Silverman, D. (1985) *Qualitative Methodology and Sociology.* Aldershot: Gower.

2
Social dimensions of assisted reproduction

MEG STACEY

The scientific revolution in human reproduction

A reproductive revolution began some 200 or more years ago when medicine joined with post-enlightenment science and when medical men (all men in those days) took over the management of childbirth – when midwifery became obstetrics. That history has been well recorded and analysed from more than one point of view (Arney, 1982; Donnison, 1977; Kitzinger, 1962; Oakley, 1976, 1984; Rich, 1977; Stacey, 1988, ch. 17; Towler and Bramall, 1986). Over the past 30 years the practice of obstetrics has become more interventionist in ways which women having a normal delivery have not always been pleased about, but for which women in trouble with their labour have had cause to be grateful.

More recently the nature of this revolution has speeded up and taken on something of a new direction. Ever since the birth of the first IVF baby in 1978, all of us have become familiar with the possibility and actuality of conception outside the womb – popularly known as 'test tube babies', although petri dishes rather than test tubes are the vessels in which sperm and egg are combined. Antenatal tests administered to pregnant women to diagnose whether the child they are carrying is impaired have become common knowledge. *In vitro* techniques can also be used to ensure that embryos placed in the womb are not carrying a hereditable disease. The possibility of genetic manipulation to remove inherited impairments is also on the agenda.

It is less than 40 years since James Watson discovered DNA – the material of which genes are constituted and wherein information about our inherited characteristics is stored. The new genetics, so christened according to Sir David Weatherall as recently as 1979 (Weatherall, 1985: 1), has opened new understandings about the transmission of life and growth. The speed of acquisition of new knowledge has been truly remarkable. In a number of named diseases geneticists now know precisely which are the genes which carry them and where they are located on the DNA. One hears news of fresh discoveries almost daily. Embryologists are constantly increasing their understanding of the beginnings of human life, of what may go wrong and, they hope, how later on they may be able to put matters right.

Between them, the new genetics and the reproductive technologies are making *a scientific revolution in human reproduction*. By that I do not mean to suggest that uncontrollable changes have been unleashed (McNeil, 1990); rather, that their very use implies the creation of totally new ideas and practices, which in principle could be taken in a variety of directions.

These developments will have consequences well beyond their immediate applications, for the new ideas and practices created are changing the culture and structure of our society. To say that birth is as much a social as a biological event is a sociological truism, although one not generally recognized, as later chapters, notably 6 and 7, make plain. Reproduction is about the future of the society as well as about the future of the species; the way reproduction is handled will inevitably affect the future, not only biologically but also socially and culturally. Reproductive techniques influence as well as reflect the basic values of societies which use them.

In this context it is astonishing that no call was made for adequate and thorough social science research before widespread application of the new techniques was proceeded with. Faith has been put in science and technology to provide solutions to problems of childlessness and of congenital impairments. The insights which social science research could offer into the probable secondary consequences (for good or ill) of the technical applications have been almost totally neglected. Nor have they been referred to in determining rules of practice or legislation to regulate practice. The role of ethics and of law has been recognized, but many matters surrounding the new human reproduction remain in the arena of uninformed opinion. This chapter aims to describe how social science has been neglected and to indicate what it can offer.

Putting the social science case

My attention was first drawn to the existence of a problem in the recognition of the social science role when I was a scientific adviser on health research bodies in the UK and Europe. Some ten or so years ago I raised the issue on a Department of Health liaison committee at a time when, in response to the new genetics, increased funding was being offered for medical genetic research. The case for parallel social science research seemed to me clear, given the obvious social component of the application of such research, particularly in relation to prenatal diagnosis. There was some recognition of the need for counselling, an application of a social-work kind, but this was seen as the limit of the relevance of the social. I failed to convince the assembled doctors and civil servants that there was an aspect to the developments which required *fundamental* social scientific analysis, initially at a theoretical level and also at an empirical level.

In the early 1980s on the European Advisory Committee

for Health Research (EACHR) of the World Health Organization (WHO) I put forward the same case. It was initially felt that my questions about assisted reproduction and prenatal diagnosis could be answered by a lawyer. The lawyer had much of value to say, but could not cover the sociological aspects. I persisted in my arguments that what was afoot was the acceleration of a *scientific revolution in human reproduction* whose social aspects were largely being neglected. My attempts were misconstrued as an attack on genetic research. That was not my aim, but to draw attention to a dangerously neglected aspect of the proposed application of science and technology. After three years I persuaded the committee to receive a scientific paper on my reasons for believing that social science research in the area of human reproduction should be encouraged in all the member countries. The paper was accepted by the committee. That year my term of office ended. My impression is that the EACHR did not pursue the issue very strongly; I was not asked back for an agendum on the topic the following year – a procedure commonly followed when a member had been making a particular contribution at the end of her/his term of office. An official WHO paper has now been published to which I will refer later.

Some 12 or more years ago a senior British microbiologist, already with a great deal of experience behind him in the new genetics, told me how worried he was about what would happen 'when the medics got hold of it'; 'they are raring to go', he said. He did not, however, call upon the social science faculty in his university to help in the issues which alarmed him, although later he agreed to talk with social scientists if they made an initiative. They did not – perhaps because cuts had so affected their strength they lacked spare capacity; it requires time for a social scientist to come to terms with the language of microbiology. However, with enthusiastic encouragement funds for more staff might have been raised.

Choosing the advisers

Nevertheless, medical practitioners were and are acutely aware of the immense responsibility using the new techniques places upon them. They were quite understandably not willing to shoulder these alone, touching as they do on areas of great sensitivity. In the absence of government action, it was the Medical Research Council (MRC) and the Royal College of Obstretricians and Gynaecologists (RCOG) who sponsored the Voluntary Licensing Authority (VLA, later to become ILA). Finally the ILA was replaced by a statutory body, the Human Fertilization and Embryology Authority (HFEA) on 1 August 1991. The licensing of centres undertaking certain activities in assisted reproduction (but not gamete intrafallopian transfer – GIFT) is now a statutory requirement, as is the licensing of donor insemination and gamete and pre-embryo storage banks.

When the VLA was first set up in 1985, five out of the 13 members were lay persons. These included a lawyer with experience of the health service, a magistrate, a theologian, an actress and author and a research psychologist who, although she was Vice President of the Health Visitors' Association, was for these purposes a 'lay' woman. Rather than using her to encourage research proposals in the psychosocial area, she was asked to write an 'explanatory note' which read like an apologia for IVF apparently designed to reduce public anxiety (VLA, 1986).

By May 1991, the number of 'lay' members had been increased. Nine members were medically qualified. Of the 11 non-medical (who included the chairperson), two were biological scientists, two were ministers of religion (one Jewish, one Christian), one a nurse-midwife; others included an ex-MP, a magistrate, an actress and author, a publisher and, for the first time, a historian, although there was no longer a social scientist.

The Warnock Committee (set up by government to

inquire into issues around human fertilization and embryology) did not include a social scientist; it did have two social workers (one psychiatric) and a psychiatrist, but no psychologist, sociologist or health economist. When the Eugenics Society (Carter, 1983) devoted their nineteenth annual symposium to developments in human reproduction and their eugenic, ethical implications they included a statistician but not a substantive social scientist.

The HFEA is the first body to include a sociologist; another member is a director of social services. The HFEA's 21 members include a wider array than was ever achieved on the ILA: 11 of the 21 are women; seven are medically qualified (covering endocrinology, genetics, general practice, obstetrics and gynaecology, psychiatry); one is a midwife; two are academic lawyers of whom one, Professor Colin Campbell, Vice Chancellor of Nottingham University, is the chairperson; the vice chair is Diana (Lady) Brittan, a JP and member of the Equal Opportunities Commission (EOC); two are ministers of religion (a bishop and a rabbi). Other members are as varied as a TV programme director, an actress, an academic educationalist and a senior official of the Bank of England. Six of the 21 were previously members of the ILA, so some continuity has been assured.

This account suggests that up to now governments and influential people have largely sought enlightenment about the potential of the changes from three sources: theology, philosophy and law. The authority and expertise of other sciences and disciplines, such as anthropology, sociology and history, for example, have not been recognized (Price, 1989: 49).

Strong beliefs, attitudes and opinions

The failure to recognize the role the social sciences could play had nothing to do with any failure to recognize the importance of the impact which the new techniques might have on our society. Some people are quite convinced that the techniques are not only a good thing, but positively wonderful; others, and for widely differing reasons, are equally convinced that they are horrifying; others again are unconvinced, wondering 'where it all may lead'. Some may still prefer 'not to know', but few who have come face to face with the new developments, or paused to think about them in any depth, remain untouched by their possibilities and what they might mean.

Strong emotions and passions are aroused: strong emotions on the part of those who want to see the new techniques applied as extensively as possible – they are sure they have something valuable to offer and are afraid of restrictions – in addition they have careers and livelihoods at stake; equally strong emotions are expressed by those who feel it is quite inappropriate to interfere in this way with the natural or the divine order; others again are more concerned about power relations in this world – they are afraid that the techniques may fall into the wrong hands and be misused, or indeed are already in the wrong hands and should not be allowed to be used at all. These two last mentioned fears are found particularly in Germany where medical experiments on human beings remain a shameful memory (Hubbard, 1986); there research on the human embryo is illegal, while in Britain we have agreed to permit it under licence for the first 14 days after conception (Embryology and Human Fertilization Act, 1990). Some feminists fear a new form of male control in the application of the technologies, pointing out the masculinist nature of both science and obstetrics (for example, Corea et al., 1985; Klein, 1989).

That strong emotions should be aroused is not really surprising. Two powerful strands come together in the scientific revolution in human reproduction. The first has to do with anxieties about science itself; the second with the crucial importance of childbirth.

A love–hate relationship with science

Much of the world as we now know it has been fashioned by science and its technological applications. In this environment technological solutions are the ones preferred for the amelioration of human problems. But while members of our society continue to give high prestige to science and scientists, we are nervous about what they do – even more nervous, perhaps, about what people who apply scientific knowledge do, especially those who produce and use 'high tech'.

The scientific mode of understanding our world and the resulting technologies have been implicated in some worrying disasters. At the environmental level one thinks of Chernobyl, that dreadful explosion of a nuclear power plant from which many people will continue to suffer for many years to come; in terms of medicine, thalidomide comes to mind, where the drug administered to expectant mothers to control morning sickness maimed their children, for the drug turned out to have the ability to modify the genes. Scientists, non-scientists and technologists themselves are increasingly worried about what our many technologies are doing to our environment and to ourselves who inhabit it. These issues have become topics for world-wide political as well as scientific summit meetings.

The fallibility of scientific and medical judgements has become apparent. No longer does a majority unequivocally believe in progress or that science is the main agent of progress. In this context debates about 'nature' versus 'science' are renewed and belief in the 'natural' is increasingly stressed. Making a similar point Frances Price (1990) refers to the work of Dorothy Nelkin, who has for years documented the declining trust both in science and the regulation of scientists and the associated demand for greater scientific accountability (Nelkin, 1979, 1984; Nelkin and Swazey, 1979).

Contradictorily, we still cling to notions of our perfectibility, or at least the possibility of improvement, or the avoidance of the more unpleasant aspects of life on this earth. 'Nature' sometimes treats us rough, produces a death-dealing or crippling disease in young children, fells men in middle age, comes up with AIDS just when we thought we had conquered the epidemic diseases. Unless we intervened one way or another, 'nature' would present some of us with many more children than we could cope with, but 'she' also renders some others of us apparently unable to conceive. Before the 'enlightenment' we might have turned to the church or to wise women or cunning men for help to alleviate such troubles, but nowadays where to turn if not to science and to those who apply the knowledge it brings?

In a useful review of public opinion surveys about biotechnology, Yoxen and Hyde (1987: 47–59) confirm that many people hold contradictory views about science and its application. As a collection of people and as individuals we are remarkably ambiguous about that major enterprise in which science seeks to unlock the secrets of the natural world and in which that knowledge is then used to produce technology which will mould the world for our greater comfort, greater power or greater control. We feel science should have an answer to everything, especially about health – and then we blame it when things go wrong. We are happy to use the many pieces of equipment which have been born out of this science, but we are also afraid that it may one day overreach itself, that perhaps it has already. At best we have a love–hate relationship with science.

Science and childbirth

Nowhere perhaps is this more clearly seen than in the case of conception and birth. The creation of renewed life still continues to cause wonder and awe in those who come close to it: a mother giving birth, a gardener watching the plants unfolding in spring. In this experience of awe I believe one can include the scientists who work on the frontiers of knowledge in the cells of plants and animals, including humans, to try to uncover what it is all about.

The continued explorations of science into how life is created and what kind of life may be created come close to areas which many think of as sacred, or as lying at the heart of nature. In this the explorations, and even more the interventions which follow them, evoke deep-seated responses which may appear irrational. The Embryology and Human Fertilization Act, 1990 was principally designed to decide whether research on the conceptus – the early beginnings of human life – should be permitted, for how long and under what limits and controls. The debate which surrounded its passage through Parliament bears witness to the wide range of opinion and the intensity of feeling that interventions in the birth process may arouse.

Part of the trouble, as Mary Warnock (1985) has pointed out, is that we are afraid of what the scientists and the doctors together have done in creating life outside the womb; we are afraid of what may be the consequences if we manipulate the conceptus. It *is* awesome; we have reason to be afraid, our fear is not altogether irrational. If what has been set afoot is, as I have suggested, a revolution in human reproduction, then profound changes may be expected to follow.

Is it really a revolution?

Am I justified in calling the changes we are experiencing a revolution (*pace* McNeil, 1990)? The addition of new members to any group is a matter of interest to many people. Attempts to control conception and the products of conception are very old; they are found in all known societies as are customs, rules and moral injunctions about whether and how these controls may be exercised. We know that abortion and infanticide have been quite commonly practised even in societies where they have been morally and legally outlawed. Abortion, whether legal or not, has been practised by women who felt it would be impossible for economic or social reasons to rear the expected child. Infanticide has been practised for the same sorts of reasons or because the baby was the wrong kind of child, perhaps disabled, but more commonly because she was a girl and not a socially more desirable boy. As matters of faith, many religions have either proscribed or circumscribed these activities. Attempts to control conception, either to prevent it or to encourage it, are also, as far as we know, as old as time and have similarly attracted religious and legal attention.

However, religious leaders, philosophers, ethicists, lawyers and governments may have made rules or pronouncements, but up until the twentieth century it seems likely that what actually happened was largely in the hands of individual couples or individual women. The control of society, church or state was largely exercised *after the event* when members were caught in contravention of the mores, rules or laws: the unmarried pregnant daughter thrown out of the house, the illegitimate grandson disinherited.

The focus of control has changed

The process whereby a new member of a society is created is intimate and personal – at least it always used to be and almost always still is. Before high technology assisted reproduction, sexual intercourse had already been separated from conception in terms of preventing the latter; now fertilization of the egg by the sperm has also been separated from sex. These are both fundamental alterations of the biological process and ones which also change social relations.

The procedures are quite different from former days when a barren woman applied for help in conceiving from, for example, a diviner or healer; such help did not involve the personal intervention of others at the moment of conception itself. The new techniques require the cooperation at that moment of third parties with appropriate skills. Conception then ceases to be a private matter between two people.

At the outset those offering assisted reproduction services could decide to whom, when and whether to make them available. In this way, the new techniques inevitably introduced an element of control at a much earlier stage in the reproductive process. This was new and greatly expanded the *social* potential of the medical techniques. The techniques thus altered the relationship of medical professionals to their patients, inevitably extending professional power and control.

However, other changes also entered the doctor–patient relationship. In procedures such as IVF, clinicians and embryologists have a mutually interdependent relationship, working together as a team (Winston, 1987: 69). The obstetrician in charge of the patient may as such have a special responsibility but I guess can be no more than *primus inter pares*. These arrangements share characteristics with many other aspects of modern medicine, but in a particularly dramatic form.

In all its aspects, even in general practice but very clearly in the hospital, modern medicine is no longer based simply on a one-to-one doctor patient relationship, as I have discussed elsewhere (Stacey, 1985). The patient now depends upon the cooperation of a great many medical and non-medical personnel. Seen in an acute form in the theatres where procedures like IVF are performed, this is also true of prenatal diagnoses, particularly those which may involve the embryo *in vitro*.

In addition, legislation has been felt necessary because of the possible abuses as well as uses to which the new techniques may be put. Thus, creating hybrids using human gametes, cloning humans and interfering with the germ line (that is, inheritable parts of the DNA) are forbidden by law.

Furthermore, the Human Fertilization and Embryology Act has not only regulated the persons who may receive assisted reproduction services but has also emphasized the importance of the whole of the team involved, including not only technicians but also counsellors. In these ways the legislation has put some limits on clinical freedom; it has also put limits on personal freedom.

The two cultures again?

In looking for reasons as to why the social sciences were ignored at the outset, that 30-year-old debate which C.P. Snow started about the 'two cultures' came to mind. So I turned it up again, along with his second thoughts (Snow, 1964; also Bishop, 1991). In his original lecture in 1959 Snow discussed the English industrial revolution and how, despite the many pains it brought in its wake, it had raised the standard of life of the bulk of the population immeasurably. As the son of a worker and the grandson of a labourer he would not have wished to return to the days before it.

In Snow's analysis, the industrial revolution was followed in the twentieth century by the 'scientific revolution', the teaming of what he called 'real science' with industry, 'no longer hit and miss, no longer the ideas of odd "inventors", but the real stuff' (1964: 29). It was following his line of reasoning that I came to refer to the new reproductive technologies as *the scientific revolution in human reproduction*, that is, the teaming of 'real science' with obstetrics.

In Snow's view, himself a scientist but also a writer, his scientific revolution would bring untold benefits, as had the industrial revolution. He berated those in the arts who lacked the courage and the vision to espouse it. But mostly he deplored the total division between the arts and the sciences whose scholars were quite unable to talk to each other and heartily despised each other. This restricted the advance of British civilization, although I do not think he used that word, and would reduce our standing in the international pecking order.

When he came to take his 'second look' in the early 1960s, he conceded that perhaps he had been wrong to speak only of two cultures, although he did not agree there were a hundred and two, or two thousand and two. He did, however, regret not having mentioned 'a putative third culture' (1964: 81), a 'mixed bag' of social sciences (1964: 70). He concluded he had unreasonably omitted these, unreasonably both because of their methodologies and because of their substantive material. He discussed their contribution somewhat, but his understanding of it did not prevent him from enthusiastically backing a 'scientific revolution which will impose changes such as none of us can foresee' (1964: 92). He did not discuss whether any or any part of those changes could be subjected to systematic analysis, what choices there might be in the way the changes worked through, which ones need not be taken as inevitable. He had not perhaps learned as much as he could have done about the illumination the social sciences might be able to bring. However, he was hinting to fellow scientists that their colleagues studying the social sciences not only might be worth talking to, but that they might even have an acceptable methodology. Had the Fellows of the Royal Society perhaps been wrong when they refused the social sciences entry in the early twentieth century? For the issue 'turns on what is to count as "evidence"' (Price, 1989: 49).

Unscientific rejection of scientific inquiry

Snow's willingness to accept in faith the unknown and profound social consequences which would follow from the twentieth century scientific industrial revolution seemed to me less than worthy of a trained scientist. Similarly I have found particularly disquieting the unscientific character of a number of scientists' pronouncements on new reproductive technology. As C.P. Snow himself was at pains to point out, a characteristic of the scientific culture is a burning desire to find out more and more about the world, its inhabitants and the universe: this is in opposition to an attitude that just accepts things because 'that's the way they are'.

When I studied life in Banbury some 40 years ago there was a core of people who took what I called a 'traditional' view of life; it was characterized by the attitude 'what was good enough for my father is good enough for me' (it was a male attitude) (Staccy, 1960). Against these 'traditionalists' was a variety of people who rejected those views and wanted changes of various kinds. Among them, as you would expect, one could number the scientists, pure and applied (Stacey, 1960). Yet I constantly hear new developments, particularly, but not only, those in the new genetics, defended on the grounds that they are 'no more than an extension of what we already have been doing for a long time, at least ever since Mendel', with the implication 'so it must be all right'. For example, while conceding that later the new genetics might raise new ethical dilemmas, Sir David Weatherall said 'Genetic screening and prenatal diagnosis have been standard procedures for many years; all our new technology will do is increase the number of diseases which can be prevented in this way' (1985: 181).

What I would have expected from him as a scientist is that he would have gone on to say something like, 'and the following clinical trials, the following social science research, the following carefully documented follow-up studies, show that on balance the procedures we have been using can be judged to have been benign; that, in terms of outcomes (or any other appropriate measures), for scientists, practitioners and patients they have been worth the physical, social, psychological and economic costs'; and perhaps adding: 'However, those researches show that in any development of the techniques the following are the aspects which will require to be carefully monitored' or some similar scientific caveat. He simply went on to discuss his own clinically inspired concerns, with a good deal of sensitivity, as one would expect, but 'common-sensically' rather than scientifically. It does seem to me that 'we've done it before so we can do it again' as a defence of any, let alone new, clinical practice is remarkably unscientific.

Times are changing: dialogue begins

The evidence is clear that social science was largely ignored at the outset of this scientific revolution in human reproduction. However, there is now evidence that, tentatively, a dialogue is beginning. The first time I noticed it was in the King's Fund Consensus Forum on screening for fetal and genetic abnormality (King's Fund, 1987). The panel included Professor Hilary Rose, who has long been working in the area of the sociology of science. In addition, the invited experts included two leading medical social scientists, Dr Sally Macintyre and Dr Martin Richards, the last a psychologist, the first a sociologist, both with extensive experience of research in human reproduction. The contribution of these three gave the consequent consensus statement a character which had hitherto been lacking.

Examining the social consequences for individuals of treatments, or analysing the long-term consequences of aggregated clinical decisions is neither the business nor the training of medical scientists. From that point of view it may not be surprising that these aspects have so often been ignored. What was refreshing about the King's Fund Consensus Statement was that it included examples of such social science concerns. They can be recognized in statements such as:

> the success of a screening programme should not be judged only by its effect on the prevalence of birth impairments, *but by its total effect on the wellbeing of women and their families*. (1987: 2, emphasis added)

In arguing for evaluation research which would scrutinize the cost and benefit of the new procedures in quantitative and monetary terms, the Consensus Statement points out that

The outcomes [of procedures], whether positive or negative, are descriptive and qualitative, and are often taken as no more than points for consideration. *The principal justification for providing screening programmes lies in such currently unquantified effects.* (1987: 6, emphasis added)

As examples of benefits, the statement mentions the provision of authoritative information, relief from uncertainty, support during a period of crisis and expansion of individual choice; potential harms include the introduction of worrying delays while confirmatory tests are conducted, distress from false positives and illusory reassurance from false negatives. Possible long-term consequences for the status and integration of disabled people are also mentioned. Finally the statement stresses the importance of monitoring all facets of outcome, difficult though this may sometimes be (1987: 11).

One is entitled to wonder why a synthesis of medical and social scientific evidence of this kind is so rarely found? The answer, of course, has to do with the utterly different and hitherto quite separate discourses of medical and social scientists.

Other signs of progress are emerging. Late in 1989 the report of the Polkinghorne Committee was published (HMSO, 1989). Its chairperson was a theologian and scientist; it also included Ian Kennedy, a lawyer with particular experience of medical accountability, and Dr Sally Macintyre, the medical sociologist already mentioned. The committee had been set up by government to advise on the use of fetal tissue resulting from abortions. The report showed a broader understanding of the issues than had hitherto been available or than is visible in the Embryology and Human Fertilization Act, 1990. I quote Gail Vines's (1990) useful summary:

[The committee] concluded that the choice of whether to donate fetal tissue for research, or for the treatment of diseases such as Parkinson's, should be the woman's whose fetus it was. Her consent should be informed and free of coercion by doctors or by financial considerations. A central clearing house would ensure that doctors seeking donations had no links with doctors or scientists making use of fetal tissue, and that no money changed hands.

Another dialogue is emerging from the ESRC initiative on the public understanding of science. One piece of work (Helen Lambert and Hilary Rose) focuses not on the public's ignorance of science, but the scientists' failure to make what they say and do salient for the public for whom it is intended.

The WHO consultation on the place of *in vitro* fertilization in infertility care (WHO, 1990) included a welcome and hitherto unusual cross-section of relevant personnel. Fifteen participants came from Europe, North America and Australia. They included representatives of gynaecologists offering IVF, women's groups, epidemiologists, sociologists, economists, health administrators and journalists. The topics covered included:

1 defining and assessing the amount of infertility in each country;
2 assessing the infertility services (paying first attention to preventive services and including assessment of social options available to infertile people, of IVF in relation to all other services available or needed and the importance of counselling and support);
3 assessment of IVF and related technologies, starting with adequate evaluation (at present unavailable) of all aspects of IVF and related technologies and second to

evaluate all direct and indirect costs of IVF;
4   planning and resource allocation, which requires bring-
     ing together all information garnered in the preceding
     exercises;
5   the provision of quality assurance;
6   ethical considerations which should first focus on the
     services provided, including equity, and on the rights of
     women and men, not just on the egg, embryo and fetus,
     and which should involve the community.

What is new about this exercise is that it has put the
provision of IVF in context of the totality of health services
and recognized the existence of its social and psychological
sequelae. In doing this the report calls for social as well as
epidemiological and clinical research. It is also encouraging
because WHO had called together medically trained IVF
practitioners and epidemiologists, along with patients and
potential patients (otherwise known as 'lay' persons) and
social scientists. These people were not only able to talk
together but to produce a report.

Multiple discourses not dichotomies

A major contribution of medical sociology has been to
demonstrate ways in which the world of some medical
practitioners and the discourses of their world differ from
the everyday language and experience of their patients and
the patients' relatives. Drawing on two separate pieces of
research, Hilary Graham and Ann Oakley (1981) have
described the quite different images of pregnancy held by
obstetricians and gynaecologists. For parental consent to
paediatric cardiac surgery, Priscilla Alderson (1990) has
demonstrated the wide gulf between the factors taken into
account by the parents and those considered by the cardiac
team.
Where they occur between doctors and patients or their

relatives, these different understandings are associated with unequal authority and power. The tragedy lies in the unnecessary personal suffering, the escalation of fear, the unnecessary antagonism and controversy which has resulted. This is the price being paid for the failure of medical science hitherto to accept either the validity of the individual patient's understanding or the authority of social science to explain what is going on. The problems are to some extent exacerbated by the still continuing male domination of many of the relevant professions. One consequence has been the failure in medical discourse to recognize women as rational as well as sentient human beings. This was where the Polkinghorne Committee was so refreshingly different. The outright opposition to the new reproductive technology by, for example, FINRRAGE (Feminist International Network for Resistance to Reproductive and Genetic Engineering) has in part been fuelled by this complex of problems.

The issues cannot be expressed in dichotomies, although they frequently are. They cannot be reduced to medical versus lay, women versus men or the informed versus the ignorant. Disputes do occur within medicine on all the topics surrounding human reproduction – some have broken out in public. There are also many different 'public' reactions: there is no monolithic 'Society' to which disputes may be referred for resolution as is sometimes proposed (see for example Bobrow and Manners, 1991). The issues relate to the totally different social context of the medical and allied scientists and practitioners and that of the patient in which each cries 'they don't understand'.

Images of assisted reproduction

There are two images of assisted reproduction available which are in stark contrast. The first is the media image, much purveyed in the early days of assisted reproduction, of a happy woman, with her partner or sometimes her obstetrician in attendance, who has just successfully given birth to a much wanted baby after years of dashed hopes. The other is the picture painted by feminists who oppose the new technologies, such as the biologist Renate Duelli Klein. She suggests, as the cover of her book puts it, 'reproductive technology fails women: it's a con' (Klein, 1989). Both cannot be right: or can they? We undoubtedly need more systematic scientific studies.

Such studies are likely to reveal that reality is much more complex than we imagine. Sandelowski et al. (1990), for example, have shown for a US sample that in people's understanding there is no simple dichotomy between the infertile and the fertile: some couples technically infertile, and failing to produce despite assistance, continue to find reason to consider themselves 'fertile'.

The IVF record

Infertility treatments such as IVF are not appropriate for all the infertile. Originally it was thought appropriate only for women with blocked tubes but the range of indications has been extended to include 'unexplained infertility'. By extracting a woman's eggs a male partner's fertility may be tested on human eggs rather than those of a hamster. Genetic investigation of the fetus for abnormalities also requires IVF – the first baby to be born in the UK following preimplantation genetic diagnosis, sex-selected to avoid genetic abnormality, was born in 1990. The uses of IVF are continually extending (ILA, 1991: 38–9, 43; Spallone, 1989: 547; WHO, 1990: summary, p. 2).

Of the involuntarily childless for whom IVF is thought appropriate, and is attempted, the success rate is not high. (Data will be given here only for IVF; in broad terms the same picture is painted for GIFT.) Of 8,790 patients receiving IVF in 1989, 1,599 became pregnant and 1,157 gave birth to at least one live baby; 1,548 babies (754 boys,

694 girls) were born in all (ILA, 1991: tab. II, p. 20; tab. XVII, p. 31). The crude live birth rate, taking all centres together, has improved from 8.6 per cent per treatment cycle in 1985 to 11.1 per cent in 1989 (ILA, 1991: 22). Although there are some variations in these rates from one centre to another, the highest live birth rate per treatment cycle noted for 1989 is 11.6 per cent (ILA, 1991: tab. IV, p. 21). The pregnancy rates, although higher than the live birth rates, are still low, being 15.4 per cent in 1989 (ILA, 1991: tab. V, p. 22).

Many women will have undergone a number of treatment cycles before they conceive and a number of these will even then lose their baby; for example, the pregnancy rate per treatment cycle is 13.9 per cent for those women undergoing their fourth IVF attempt, but the live birth rate is only 9.3 per cent. The number of live births per treatment cycle declined sharply after five attempts; the success rate at the eleventh or more attempt fell to 2.3 per cent (ILA, 1991: tab. XIV, p. 29). Live birth rates also declined sharply in women over 40, falling from 14.1 per cent per cycle for those less than 25 years old to 4.5 per cent for those aged 40–44 and to nil for those over 45 (ILA, 1991: 27, 29).

Babies carried to term may be born dead or survive only a brief time. In 1989 the perinatal death rate (that is, the baby was stillborn or died within a week) after IVF was 17.0 compared to 26.4 in 1988 (ILA, 1990: 18, 20). This is over twice the national average for perinatal deaths (8.3 in 1989).

Over a quarter (26.8 per cent) of the pregnancies achieved after IVF were twins, triplets or more, compared with around 1 per cent of unassisted pregnancies. The risk of a multiple pregnancy increases with the number of eggs or embryos transferred (ILA, 1991: 18). 'Compared with singletons, babies from triplet and higher order births are about six times more likely to be stillborn, and live-born babies are ten times more likely to die during their first year' (ILA, 1991: 38). According to the national study of triplet and higher order births, in 1989 65 sets of triplets and 3 of quadruplets were born following IVF (ILA, 1991: 43). Almost half of the quadruplets or higher order births occurred before 32 weeks' gestation compared with a quarter of the triplets and less than a tenth of the twins. Over half the quads and just over a quarter of the triplets had very low birth weights: under 1,500 g – such low weights do not bode well for a child.

In 1988, 13 IVF children were born with congenital abnormalities (ILA, 1990: 25). The more thorough recording used in 1989 shows that the true figure was probably higher than this. Thirty-two of the IVF babies that year were recorded as born impaired; 28 had congenital abnormalities and four, chromosomal syndromes (ILA, 1991: 26). This is twice the national rate. Abnormalities such as these are more likely in multiple births.

The social meaning of the figures

What these data can mean in social terms for the woman who bears twins, triplets or more, for her partner and for the children growing up was the subject of the welcome government-funded research project mentioned earlier (Botting et al., 1990). This and other work (for example, Botting et al., 1987; see also Chapter 5 in this volume) suggests that discussion of the high risks of multiparity in procedures such as IVF and GIFT should not be confined to clinical cases but should extend to the social aspects surrounding the birth and care of the children.

So we see that women whose conception is assisted are liable to all the troubles which accompany any pregnancy, and more in addition. Nevertheless, since the beginning of assisted conception to the end of 1988 something like 2,000 fit babies had been born. Having a healthy baby is the outcome which is of interest to women and couples who have difficulty in conceiving. As Dame Mary Donaldson, the ILA chairperson, has refreshingly put it, 'the "take-home baby" rate . . . is the one figure the couple really want to know'.

Nevertheless, it remains a comment on the different focus of the professional and the patient that over the years the ILA reports have said a good deal more about *pregnancy* rates than they have about *live birth* rates. The professional arguments that many embryos fertilized as a result of ordinary sexual intercourse do not implant and mature, while possibly scientifically accurate, does not make much sense in the discourse of the patients. Such failures, mostly unnoticed and unrecorded and so non-existent in the woman's experience, happen after making love; the IVF losses follow many months, indeed years, of effort and pain. Even a miscarriage of which a woman is aware has a quite different connotation from that. Steinberg (1990) has analysed extensively the ways in which the women who will bear the child tend to disappear from accounts of IVF procedures and outcomes.

Masculinist bias

Perhaps I may illustrate this point by quoting from a male obstetrician who is aware of the masculinist tendencies of those who treat using IVF. Professor Robert Winston runs the unit at Hammersmith. He finds 'a kind of macho appeal' which is associated with *in vitro* fertilization very distasteful. He goes on:

> So often, when we go to an international meeting to talk about some aspect of infertility, the immediate question colleagues ask is how many IVF pregnancies have you got? If none, it is assumed you can't be much good at reproduction. (1987: 75)

Nevertheless, he is not himself entirely immune:

> *In vitro* fertilization is a disturbing and demanding

treatment. It frequently causes immense distress to the couple undergoing it. It is also physically difficult and very time-consuming. Indeed, the woman usually has to give up work during treatment and, unless she is prepared to travel, may have to live temporarily in digs or a hotel during the treatment cycle so that she may be 'on call'. Moreover, the stress on the male partner is not to be belittled. He is required to give support and encouragement at all times and, most important, needs to produce semen at short notice in hospital premises in circumstances which are very dispiriting. Because of this, it is not unknown for men in these circumstances to find it impossible to get an erection, let alone ejaculate. (1987: 76–7)

Thirty-nine words for the woman's difficulties (and nothing about women who struggle to keep on with their jobs) and sixty-five words for the men's, although it is the woman who bears the brunt of the treatment throughout.

Not only is Robert Winston a man but he lives and works in a masculinist world. The science which made IVF possible is a male-dominated science; it is not neutral as to the problems it selects for research or its mode of handling them (Harding, 1986; Rose, 1983, 1987). Obstetric practice in this country, despite an increasing number of women, and of independently minded women, is also still dominated by men.

What is needed is a recognition that the nature of the stresses and strains to which the woman and her partner will be subjected are capable of scientific analysis. A variety of kinds of evidence of what the procedures mean in practice now exists. Price (1990) cites the psychological studies (Johnston et al., 1987; Shaw and Johnston, 1987) of stress and anxiety associated with IVF. Few studies have been derived from publicly funded social science research. Botting et al.'s work (1990) on multiple births is something of an exception. Such analyses, taken with a good dose of the

scientific spirit which makes it possible to swallow unpalat-
able findings, would go a long way to overcome the
unnecessary, and I am sure unintended, consequences like
the depersonalization of women in IVF procedures (Steinberg, 1990).

Women's views

In accounts which have come from the women's movement
(for example, Klein, 1989) the overwhelming nature of the
programmes is described. A woman finds her life taken over
by medical procedures. These accounts amply bear out
Robert Winston's comment when he says the preliminary
medical treatment 'may be quite involved . . . surgery to
free the ovaries and many other distressing tests such as
hormone studies, with daily blood sampling and ultrasound'
(1987: 65). Women report unpleasant side effects from the
drug regimes to induce superovulation, that is, the production of more than one egg at a time (Klein, 1989; Spallone,
1989: 58).

The accounts by Maggie Humm (Klein, 1989: 35–45) and
her husband, Peter (Klein, 1989: 51–8) of her, ultimately
successful, attempts to become pregnant using a drug regime
in the mid-1970s illustrate this. She had severe side effects,
including emergency hospitalization. Their accounts also
testify to the implications of the 'macho appeal' referred to
by Robert Winston for a woman undergoing treatment. Her
husband who had problems which he no doubt shares with
many men had increased difficulty because he was committed to the liberation of women and recognized how the
'macho' environment enhanced the pain his wife endured.

It is important that accounts of this kind should be
available, from women whose treatment has succeeded and
those for whom it has not worked – this was one of the
refreshing aspects of the 1990 WHO conference. However, I
do not think Renate Klein is justified in concluding from

these and other experiences of women that the 'technologies don't work, but we are led to believe they do; they are anti-woman; they are dangerous and dehumanizing in their theory and application' (1989: 279). The truth, which it is important that social scientists should be given a chance to unravel, is much more complex than that. Social life *is* very complex.

Problems with norms

Technology as practised changes expectations

At one time there was a normative expectation shared by all pregnant women that some children would be born disabled. This has changed to the expectation that a woman is responsible for having tests to establish the fitness of the fetus. Added to this, as things stand, if tests suggest the fetus is damaged in some way the norm now is that she should abort it. From a situation, only a quarter of a century ago and much more recently in some countries, when abortion was illegal except to save a woman's life, we have now reached a situation where the normative expectation is that a woman should abort a less-than-perfect fetus.

Evidence from the United States suggests that women who receive an adverse prenatal diagnosis request abortion, including those whose religion proscribes that solution. With hindsight, many British mothers of severely handicapped adults would have aborted had they known (Simms, 1986). When the promises of genetic manipulation are fulfilled, a mother will have the alternative of accepting manipulation for the embryo. The more immediate prospect is that, in cases like Duchenne muscular dystrophy, for example, a woman could agree to the use of *in vitro* techniques so that only an unaffected embryo is replaced in her womb (Walton, 1989).

Barbara Katz Rothman (1988) in her research on a sample

of American women found that nowadays pregnancies are treated as tentative in case prenatal tests should reveal an impairment and the pregnancy be terminated. An open mind and some anxiety about the outcome has been replaced by this new norm of the tentative, although assurance of perfection still cannot be offered.

Prenatal tests have increased women's choices. But as Rothman and others have pointed out, increased choices may remove other choices. The opportunity to avoid bearing an impaired child can also increase the restrictions pregnant women experience. The choice to control the quality of the child may lead to loss of the choice (and in the end perhaps of the ability) simply to accept children as they are (Finger, 1984; Rapp, 1984; Rothman, 1988; Saxton, 1984). This may have consequences for the acceptance of all sorts of variations which children may present.

There will always be variations in human beings; there will always be handicap resulting from uncontrollable congenital conditions, from later illness or accident. We need to keep the new developments in context. Relatively few birth defects are genetically inherited. Not only are there new mutations to bear in mind, but to 'make matters even more unpredictable, many congenital malformations – ranging from cleft palate to spina bifida – probably have some genetic basis, complexly intermeshed with environmental factors' (Birke et al., 1990: 175).

What Lord Walton did not mention when supporting embryo research in his eloquent speech about Duchenne muscular dystrophy in the House of Lords (Walton, 1989) (although the statistics he did give were impeccable) was that some 20–30 per cent of muscular dystrophy cases are new mutations which could not be detected by a family history of the disease (Birke et al., 1990; Knox and Lancashire, 1991: 195; Vlad, 1987, personal communication). 'Screening every pregnant woman for the disease would be prohibitively expensive, as well as dangerous' (Birke et al., 1990: 195). There is already evidence that the supposed eradication of the cause of impairment results in the drying up of research which might benefit survivors (Kaufert and Kaufert, 1984: 616).

Reinforcing some norms

In a society where a dominant norm is that couples should conceive and be fruitful, involuntary childlessness is a great sorrow. Its impact upon men and upon women is probably different. For some men it seems important that 'his' woman should bear 'his' child. There have always been women who have not wished to accept the wife–mother role, women and couples who wish to remain childless. 'Childlessness' should be distinguished from infertility (Crowe, 1990: 38; Pfeffer, 1987: 83); the latter is a medical construct (WHO, 1990). There are strong sanctions exercised to encourage a married woman to conceive and bear children (Pfeffer, 1987; Pfeffer and Woolett, 1983). A generally accepted view is that for a married woman to be barren is a denial of her womanhood. Sanctions are also exercised against unmarried women who want to bear children (Barrett and McIntosh, 1982; Macintyre, 1976a, 1976b). However, the wish to become a mother is not confined to married or heterosexual women: it is shared by single and lesbian women (Klein, 1984: 382–90; Lewin, 1985). The feelings of distress of the infertile are real (Pfeffer and Woolett, 1983). It is reasonable that medical practitioners should wish to relieve this condition. Paradoxically, the distress is enhanced by the long drawn out, and often unsuccessful, process of infertility treatment.

A consequence of pursuing any medical route to the solution of infertility is to reinforce the high normative value already placed upon biological procreation. It also reinforces the family built by biological reproduction to the exclusion of other child-rearing arrangements. Parents and children in families built in other ways, such as fostering or adoption, have always realized that socially these modes are seen as second best (Kirk, 1964). Fewer children are available for adoption nowadays but varieties of access to children, through shared care, for example, have also been devised. The more the biological mode is stressed the greater this tendency to stigmatize families other than the biological may be likely to become (but see also Chapter 6 by Erica Haimes).

Counter-revolutionary aspects: conservative use of technologies

The technologies, revolutionary as they are, could be used in so many ways. In practice they are being used conservatively, even reactionarily – and without initiating a quest for research evidence. Apparently some notion of 'the normal family' is being used (Haimes, 1990). There have been immense changes in marriage and the family over recent years. Something like one in three marriages now ends in divorce; the incidence of stepchildren is increasing; illegitimacy no longer stigmatizes as it once did; people have been experimenting with other modes of child-rearing than the nuclear family; the nuclear family itself has acquired a bad record for violence, especially against women and children; in our multi-cultural society many people are of mixed 'race'.

For the first time the ILA has mentioned the 'needs of ethnic minorities'. The 1991 report recommends that 'an appropriate ethnic range of sperm' should be available. Reference is made to the 'welfare of the resulting child' and to the Race Relations Act. There are complex social and cultural issues hidden here to which no overt reference is made, nor is relevant research called for by the ILA.

The model which is being used in framing regulations and admitting persons to IVF and similar programmes is one of the white, middle class, stable, nuclear family. Why? In whose interest is that? The Human Fertilization and Embryology Act, 1990, includes a child's need for a father as a criterion for assisted reproduction. Yet research evidence shows that the self-perception of children in fatherless families, whether heterosexual or lesbian, is not different from that in fathered families (Golombok and Rust, 1986; Golombok et al., 1983). Any problems which fatherless families encounter derive from secondary social and economic privation, not from the absence of a father *per se*.

Conservative, but changing the structure and culture

The new reproductive technologies have already made changes in our kinship system. The Human Fertilization and Embryology Act includes new definitions of what is a father and what a mother to accommodate the changes brought about by conception outside the womb. For medical reasons (not adultery) a wife may now carry a child whose genetic father is not her husband; she may carry a child whose egg was given her by another; if she cannot carry a child another woman may do it for her – the surrogate or carry-mother (Zipper and Sevenhuijsen, 1987). Many questions arise from this state of affairs, including those of the genetic identity of the resultant children (Haimes, 1990; see also Chapter 6 below).

In the debate on the Human Fertilization Bill, their Lordships expressed great anxiety about the possibility of eldest sons who were not genetically connected being able to inherit a title. They were greatly alarmed to learn that (gamete donation apart) geneticists reckon that already 20 per cent of children are not genetically related to their fathers. New social understandings are being acquired.

Nor can we ignore the socioeconomic environment in which the developments are taking place, specifically the effect of health care markets on which of the involuntarily childless may receive assisted reproduction and under what conditions. Furthermore, there is a great deal of opinion, much fear, and little systematic research into the possibilities and social effects of trade in body parts, embryos, ova from cadavers and the like. Such trade is looked at askance in the UK where legislation proscribes it, but is commonly accepted in the United States where health is predominantly provided within a capitalist, profit-making, rather than a welfare framework.

There is a tendency, from which medical practitioners are not exempt, to think of 'society' as something 'out there' which constrains our actions. This is partly true, but the matter is more complicated than that. Each of us everyday is recreating our society by our words and actions or lack of actions. Those in positions of power and authority, including medical practitioners, have more space to actualize their visions. In doing this they may initiate changes which go beyond those they had in mind.

Conclusion

This chapter has argued that the scientific revolution in human reproduction has set afoot changes which are likely to have extensive ramifications. These changes will not happen by themselves, nor are they predetermined. They and their characteristics will not derive directly from the technologies, but from the ways in which those technologies are administered and controlled. People with power and authority will have direct responsibility for the changes; the acceptance or rejection of the applications by ordinary people will also play a part.

Replace the 'slippery slope' by systematic analysis

There has been a great deal of talk about 'slippery slopes' in all the discussions surrounding assisted reproduction and prenatal diagnosis. The analogy suggests that we do not and cannot understand what may be the consequences of any moves that may be made in this new world that is developing. It also suggests that all such moves are necessarily down hill, and that what is at the bottom has to be bad. The fear which people are expressing when they use this analogy requires to be named and analysed. Whereas in truth, although social science along with other sciences has no crystal ball, social scientific analysis can offer some enlightenment. It can describe and analyse changes which have already taken place, examine – using theory as guidance – what other consequences there might be, distinguish the state of affairs common sense considers we have now from what empirically exists, and relate proposed changes to that.

My aim has been to persuade scientists from other disciplines, medical practitioners, policy makers and interested citizens that there are social facets of this scientific revolution in human reproduction which can usefully be researched; that it is worth paying attention to the research that has already been done. This is not to suggest that social scientists can provide all the answers. What they can offer is some greater understanding of what the new technologies involve so that debate and decision making may be better informed.

Note

My gratitude to the EACHR of WHO EURO for the grant to hold a seminar of experts in preparation for the 1988 paper and my gratitude also to the seminar participants. Thanks are also due to all co-authors of this book for their helpful comments on earlier drafts of this chapter and for their invaluable help in the editing of the book itself.

Bibliography

Alderson, D.P. (1990) *Choosing for Children: Parents' Consent to Surgery*. Oxford: Oxford University Press.

Arney, W.R. (1982) *Power and the Profession of Obstetrics*. Chicago and London: University of Chicago Press.

Barrett, M. and McIntosh, M. (1982) *The Anti-social Family*. London: Verso.

Birke, L., Himmelweit, S. and Vines, G. (1990) *Tomorrow's Child: Reproductive Technologies in the 90s*. London: Virago.

Bishop, M.G.H. (1991) ' "A new cageful of ferrets" – medicine and the "two cultures" debate of the 1950s', *Journal of the Royal Society of Medicine*, 84(11): 637–9.

Bobrow, M. and Manners, E. (1991) 'Social consequences of advances in the clinical application of genetics'. Paper presented to the Fullbright International Colloquium on the Social Consequences of Life and Death under High Technology Medicine, Burnham Beeches, Bucks, UK, 14–16 December (mimeo).

Botting, B., MacDonald Davies, I. and Macfarlane, A. (1987) 'Recent trends in the incidence of multiple births and associated mortality', *Archives of the Diseases of Childhood*, 62: 941–50.

Botting, B., Macfarlane, A. and Price, F. (1990) *Three, Four or More: a Study of Triplets and Higher Order Births*. HMSO: London.

Carter, C.O. (ed.) (1983) *Developments in Human Reproduction and the Eugenic, Ethical Implications: Proceedings of the Nineteenth Annual Symposium of the Eugenics Society London 1982*. London: Academic Press.

Corea, G., Klein, R.D. et al. (1985) *Man-made Women*. London: Hutchinson.

Crowe, C. (1990) 'Whose mind over whose matter? Women, *in vitro* fertilization and the development of scientific knowledge', in M. McNeil, I. Varcoe and S. Yearley (eds), *The New Reproductive Technologies*. Basingstoke: Macmillan, pp. 27–57, 281–97.

Donnison, J. (1977) *Midwives and Medical Men: a History of Inter-professional Rivalries and Women's Rights*. London: Heinemann; 2nd edn 1988, Historical Publications.

Finger, A. (1984) 'Claiming all of our bodies: reproductive rights and disabilities', in R. Arditti, R.D. Klein and S. Minden (eds), *Test-tube Women: What Future for Motherhood?* London and Boston: Pandora, pp. 281–97.

Franklin, S. (1990) 'Deconstructing "desperateness": the social construction of infertility in popular representations of new reproductive technologies', in M. McNeil, I. Varcoe and S.

Yearley (eds), *The New Reproductive Technologies*. Basingstoke: Macmillan, pp. 200–29.

Golombok, S. and Rust, J. (1986) 'The Warnock Report and single women. What about the children?', *Journal of Medical Ethics*, 12(4): 182–6.

Golombok, S., Spencer, A. and Rutter, M. (1983) 'Children in lesbian and single-parent households: psychosexual and psychiatric appraisal', *Journal of Child Psychology and Psychiatry*, 24: 551–72.

Graham, H. and Oakley, A. (1981) 'Competing ideologies of reproduction: medical and maternal perspectives on pregnancy', in H. Roberts (ed.), *Women, Health and Reproduction*. London: Routledge and Kegan Paul, pp. 50–74.

Haimes, E. (1990) 'Recreating the family?', in M. McNeil, I. Varcoe and S. Yearley (eds), *The New Reproductive Technologies*. Basingstoke: Macmillan, pp. 154–72.

Harding, S. (1986) *The Science Question in Feminism*. Milton Keynes: Open University Press.

HMSO (1989) *Review of the Guidance on the Research Uses of Fetuses and Fetal Material* ('Polkinghorne Report'). London: HMSO, Cm 762.

Hubbard, R. (1986) 'Eugenics and prenatal testing', *International Journal of Health Services*, 16: 227–42.

ILA (1990) *The Fifth Report of the Interim Licensing Authority for Human In Vitro Fertilization and Embryology*. London: ILA.

ILA (1991) *The Sixth Report of the Interim Licensing Authority for Human In Vitro Fertilization and Embryology*. London: ILA.

Johnston, M., Shaw, R. and Bird, D. (1987) 'Test-tube baby procedures: stress and judgements under uncertainty', *Psychology and Health*, 1: 25–38.

Kaufert, P.L. and Kaufert, J.M. (1984) 'Methodological and conceptual issues in measuring the long term impact of disability: the experience of poliomyelitis patients in Manitoba', *Social Science and Medicine*, 19: 609–18.

King's Fund (1987) *Screening For Fetal and Genetic Abnormality*. King's Fund Forum Consensus Statement. London: King's Fund Centre.

Kirk, D. (1964) *Shared Fate: a Theory of Adoption and Mental Health*. London: Free Press of Glencoe, Collier-Macmillan.

Kitzinger, S. (1962) *The Experience of Childbirth*. London: Gollancz.

Klein, R.D. (1984) 'Doing it ourselves: self-insemination', in R. Arditti, R.D. Klein and S. Minden (eds), *Test-tube Women: What Future for Motherhood?* London and Boston: Pandora, pp. 382–90.

Klein, R.D. (1989) *Infertility: Women Speak Out*. London: Pandora.

Knox, E.G. and Lancashire, R.J. (1991) *The Epidemiology of Congenital Malformations*. London: HMSO.

Lewin, E. (1985) 'By design: reproductive strategies and the meaning of motherhood', in H. Homans (ed.), *The Sexual Politics of Reproduction*. Aldershot: Gower, pp. 123–38.

Macintyre, S. (1976a) 'To have or to have not – promotion and prevention of childbirth in gynaecological work', in M. Stacey (ed.), *The Sociology of the National Health Service*, Sociological Review Monograph 22. Keele: University of Keele, pp. 176–93, 150–73, 1–26.

Macintyre, S. (1976b) ' "Who wants babies?" The social construction of "instincts" ', in D.L. Barker and S. Allen (eds), *Sexual Divisions and Society: Process and Change*. London: Tavistock, pp. 150–73.

McNeil, M. (1990) 'Reproductive technologies: a new terrain for the sociology of technology', in M. McNeil, I. Varcoe and S. Yearley (eds), *The New Reproductive Technologies*. Basingstoke: Macmillan.

Nelkin, D. (ed.) (1979) *Controversy: Politics of Technical Decisions*. London: Sage.

Nelkin, D. (1984) *Science as Intellectual Property: Who Controls Research?* London: Collier Macmillan.

Nelkin, D. and Swazey, J.P. (1979) 'Science and social control: controversies over research on violence', in H. Skoie (ed.), *1979: 5 Scientific Expertise and the Public: Conference Proceedings*. Oslo: Institute for Studies in Higher Education, The Norwegian Research Council for Science and the Humanities, pp. 208–22.

Oakley, A. (1976) 'Wisewomen and medicine man: changes in the management of childbirth', in J. Mitchell and A. Oakley (eds), *The Rights and Wrongs of Women*. Harmondsworth: Penguin, pp. 304–78.

Oakley, A. (1984) *The Captured Womb: A History of the Medical Care of Pregnant Women*. Oxford and New York: Basil Blackwell.

Pfeffer, N. (1987) 'Artificial insemination, *in vitro* fertilization and the stigma of infertility', in M. Stanworth (ed.), *Reproductive Technologies: Gender, Motherhood and Medicine*. Cambridge: Polity Press, pp. 81–97.

Pfeffer, N. and Woolett, A. (1983) *The Experience of Infertility*. London: Virago.

Price, F. (1989) 'Establishing guidelines: regulation and the clinical management of infertility', in R. Lee and D. Morgan (eds), *Birthrights: Law and Ethics at the Beginnings of Life*. London: Routledge, pp. 37–54.

Price, F. (1990) 'The management of uncertainty in obstetric practice: ultrasonography, *in vitro* fertilization and embryo transfer', in M. McNeil, I. Varcoe and S. Yearley (eds), *The New Reproductive Technologies*. Basingstoke: Macmillan, pp. 123–53.

Rapp, R. (1984) 'XYL0: a true story', in R. Arditti, R.D. Klein and S. Minden (eds), *Test-tube Women: What Future for Motherhood?* London and Boston: Pandora, pp. 313–28.

Rich, A. (1977) *Of Woman Born: Motherhood as Experience and Institution*. London: Virago.

Rose, H. (1983) 'Hand, brain and heart: towards a feminist epistemology of the natural sciences', *Signs: a Journal of Women in Culture and Society*, 9(1): 73–90.

Rose, H. (1987) 'Victorian values in the test tube: the politics of reproductive science and technology', in M. Stanworth (ed.), *Reproductive Technologies: Gender, Motherhood and Medicine*. Cambridge: Polity Press, pp. 151–73.

Rothman, B.K. (1988) *The Tentative Pregnancy: Prenatal Diagnosis and the Future of Motherhood*. London: Pandora.

Sandelowski, M., Holditch-Davis, D. and Harris, B.G. (1990) 'Living the life: explanations of infertility', *Sociology of Health and Illness*, 12(2): 195–215.

Saxton, M. (1984) 'Born and unborn: the implications of reproductive technologies for people with disabilities', in R. Arditti, R.D. Klein and S. Minden (eds), *Test-tube Women: What Future for Motherhood?* London and Boston: Pandora, pp. 298–312.

Shaw, P. and Johnston, M. (1987) 'Couples awaiting IVF: Counselling needs, emotional and relational problems'. Paper presented to the Society for Reproductive and Infant Psychology annual conference, Edinburgh, September.

Simms, M. (1986) 'Informed dissent: the views of some mothers of severely mentally handicapped young adults', *Journal of Medical Ethics*, 12(2): 72–4.

Snow, C.P. (1964) *The Two Cultures: and A Second Look*. London: Cambridge University Press.

Spallone, P. (1989) *Beyond Conception: the New Politics of Reproduction*. Basingstoke: Macmillan.

Stacey, M. (1960) *Tradition and Change: a Study of Banbury*. London: Oxford University Press.

Stacey, M. (1985) 'Medical ethics and medical practice – a social science view', *Journal of Medical Ethics*, 11(1): 14–18.

Stacey, M. (1988) *The Sociology of Health and Healing: a Textbook*. London: Unwin Hyman.

Steinberg, D.L. (1990) 'The depersonalization of women through the administration of *in vitro* fertilization', in M. McNeil, I. Varcoe and S. Yearley (eds), *The New Reproductive Technologies*. Basingstoke: Macmillan, pp. 74–122.

Towler, J. and Bramall, J. (1986) *Midwives in History and Society*. London: Croom Helm.

Vines, G. (1990) 'Women are still kept out in the embryo debate', *Correspondent*, February, p. 37.

VLA (1986) *The First Report of the Voluntary Licensing Authority for Human In Vitro Fertilization and Embryology*. London: VLA.

VLA (1989) *The Fourth Report of the Voluntary Licensing Authority for Human In Vitro Fertilization and Embryology*. London: VLA.

Walton, Lord (1989) *Hansard Lords* 10/12/89, cols 1051–6.

Warnock, M. (1985) *A Question of Life: The Warnock Report on Human Fertilization and Embryology*. Oxford: Basil Blackwell.

Weatherall, D.J. (1985) *The New Genetics and Clinical Practice*. Oxford: Oxford University Press.

WHO (1990) 'Consultation on the Place of *in vitro* Fertilization in Infertility Care', *Summary Report*. Copenhagen: World Health Organization Regional Office for Europe.

Winston, R.M.L. (1987) '*In vitro* fertilization: practice, prospects and problems', in P. Byrne (ed.), *Medicine in Contemporary Society: King's College Studies 1986–7*. London: King Edward's Hospital Fund for London, pp. 64–83.

Yoxen, E. and Hyde, B. (1987) *The Social Impact of Biotechnology*. Luxembourg: Office for Official Publications of the European Communities.

Zipper, J. and Sevenhuijsen, S. (1987) 'Surrogacy: feminist notions of motherhood reconsidered', in M. Stanworth (ed.), *Reproductive Technologies: Gender, Motherhood and Medicine*. Cambridge: Polity Press, pp. 118–38.

3

From private patients to privatization (a brief history of services for the treatment of infertility in England and Wales during the twentieth century)

NAOMI PFEFFER

The National Health Service (NHS) was set up in Britain in 1949 in order to break the cash nexus between sickness and medicine, to divorce health care from the ability to pay. However, in Britain today, most women who try to become pregnant through the new reproductive technologies such as IVF and GIFT, have to pay for it. According to the Sixth Report of the Interim Licensing Authority for Human *In Vitro* Fertilization and Embryology (ILA, 1991), only three IVF centres are wholly funded by the NHS, 19 make use of some NHS facilities or receive partial funding from the NHS and charge the patient for all or part of the cost of treatment, and 28 are wholly private centres.[1]

Financial considerations are rarely absent from discussions of the new reproductive technologies. Doctors and health service managers debate among themselves 'trade-off' values to the NHS – is it better to spend money on IVF than on chemotherapy – and individuals – how much of their post-tax income are people prepared to pay to have a child (which assumes that infertility patients are employed).[2] The *Independent* newspaper has published two editions of *How to Choose a Test-tube Baby Clinic*, a guide for women seeking IVF, which rates centres according to costs, accessibility, convenience and 'take home' baby rates, criteria which convey the impression that IVF clinics are supermarkets which sell motherhood. Modifications to 'test tube' technology are proclaimed a boon to patients not because they offer a greater chance of parenthood, or are safer than other procedures used by clinicians, but because they cost less.[3] One English IVF clinic succumbed to a hostile press and abandoned its offer of credit facilities for patients, a marketing ploy that equated IVF with consumer durables such as videos and stereo equipment.[4] Indeed, money has become synonymous with involuntary childlessness to the extent that lack of it has been incorporated into the aetiology of infertility; being broke is now accepted as a cause of involuntary childlessness. A newspaper article headlined 'Wife stole for test tube op', reported the trial in a magistrate's court of a 'desperate' woman who had stolen money from her boss in order to pay for a 'test-tube' operation 'so she could have a baby'. With the cash, but not without it, she was able to become pregnant.[5]

The issue of value for money in infertility treatment has been taken up by investigative journalists who have produced television programmes and written newspaper articles pointing out that, as some IVF clinics rarely manage to effect a pregnancy, infertile women and men are handing over large sums of money and getting nothing in return.[6] The 1990 report of the ILA warned clinics where patients stand little if any chance of becoming mothers that they were at risk of losing their licence to manipulate human embryos, a penalty which would effectively force them to shut up shop.[7] And the Human Fertilization and Embryology Authority (HFEA) which, in August 1991, replaced the ILA, may also refuse a licence to clinics with a dismal 'take home baby rate'.

The concern over the ways in which infertile women and men are vulnerable to exploitation is of recent origin. It represents another chapter in the long relationship between money, social status and the medical treatment of involuntary childlessness, albeit this time written in the language of consumerism.[8] Although free treatment has been provided to pregnant women and nursing mothers in Britain during most of the twentieth century, and, since 1949, medical treatment has been available free at the point of use from the NHS, the cash nexus has always been an important factor in determining who can obtain medical treatment for infertility. The medical procedures which infertile women and men undergo may have changed, but in Britain, they are as dependent as ever on the private medical sector.[9]

Why is money central to the medical treatment of infertility in Britain? Some people have argued that infertile women and men should pay for treatment because being unable to have a child is not an illness.[10] Assisted reproduction techniques have been excluded from medical insurance schemes on these grounds although the routine investigation of infertility – finding out whether there is something medically wrong – is covered by them. The counter-argument is that involuntary childlessness is so stressful that it damages people's mental health. Infertility treatment is represented as preventive medicine, a sort of psychiatric prophylactic. Another tack taken is that if the NHS treats people who bring their illness upon themselves, for example, by smoking and alcohol abuse, why should it not help the infertile, who have 'normal' human instincts but are unwitting victims of a malfunctioning reproductive system.

The debate about what constitutes an 'illness' and whether infertility is one masks the real reason why people have to pay for infertility treatment in Britain. The interplay between two powerful interest groups – gynaecologists and successive British governments – has sustained the cash nexus in infertility treatment throughout this century. The economic significance of operations provides a key to understanding attitudes and practices within the speciality of gynaecology.[11] Yet the issues around infertility treatment are not identical to those relating to elective gynaecological interventions such as hysterectomies.[12] For although services for the investigation and treatment of both infertility and menstrual disorders are grounded in the political economy of gynaecology and concepts of gender, additionally infertility engages with the thorny political issues of fertility control and population policy.

This chapter places the new reproductive technologies in a national historical context, in order to demonstrate the value of this approach. Britain serves as an exemplar; the history discussed below is set out not to delineate a rule but to advocate a methodological approach. For only history can explain why, for example, German law prohibits research on human embryos yet its medical insurance schemes will finance IVF; why in the United States, no statutory regulatory body has been set up to develop guidelines on the manipulation of human embryos in research and treatment, and there is no Federal funding for either of them; and why in Britain the manipulation of human embryos is controlled tightly by a statutory authority – the HFEA – which replaced a voluntary one – the ILA – as regulator of a medical practice found largely in the private sector.[13]

Pro- and antinatalism in Britain

All governments have a policy on the regulation of size and composition of populations – immigration and emigration are obvious mechanisms – but the extent to which it is made explicit varies according to national social and political considerations.[14] With very few exceptions, British governments have demonstrated a reluctance to support openly interventions that might be interpreted as pro- or antinatalist. Not one British government has actively promoted a policy enabling women to have or not have children, because I suggest, doing so would be tantamount to admitting that it had a population policy. According to British political thought, it is acceptable sometimes for doctors to manage women's fertility on health but never on population grounds.

It may be considered acceptable for doctors to manage women's fertility, but a British government may jeopardize its electoral majority by a too obvious connection with their practice. British governments began to be drawn into the regulation of fertility during the nineteenth century, as the state gradually replaced the church as legal but not moral arbiter on matters touching on sexuality.[15] However, following the widening of the franchise in 1918, all political parties have had to negotiate the diverse opinions of the electorate on fertility control. And since 1932, with the exception of the years of the Second World War, Britain has been governed by a minority government; there have always been more people against a government than for it. Catholic organizations with names such as the 'Southwark Parents and Electors Association' have persistently reminded politicians of the intimate relationship between policies relating to fertility and an electoral majority. Another important consideration for British governments is the mainland's unhappy relationship with Northern Ireland; almost the only issues on which Irish protestant and catholic politicians are prepared to unite are legal abortion and the manipulation of human embryos, which they both oppose. Religious considerations are not the only factors which discourage British governments from developing policies and spending public money on services that intervene into intimate and private aspects of people's lives. I am thinking here of ideas about 'rights', the freedom of the individual versus the collectivity, the significance of the family and male sensibilities that inform much government policy.[16] As a result, in Britain, political parties have deemed it wise to adopt the 'ostrich position' whenever issues relating to fertility raise their ugly head.[17]

Before the Human Fertilization and Embryology Act (1990), no British government had taken the lead on a legal instrument that touched on the technology of fertility control. Instead, legislation has been introduced into Parliament as a result of successful lobbying by powerful pressure groups, who adopt one of two strategies. Either they approach individual Members of Parliament – amendments to the abortion law have been introduced in Parliament by private members and the success of the 1967 Act which liberalized abortion, owed much to the scandal that followed the Thalidomide tragedy – or the executive – the history of family planning provides many examples of this.[18]

Legislation or a regulation that makes a service or technique relating to fertility control available to women, is rarely followed by resources sufficient to meet the new demand. After the abortion law was liberalized in 1967, extra hospital beds, nurses and doctors were not provided to meet the increased demand for gynaecologists' attention within the NHS. Inevitably, many women suffered; those on waiting lists for other gynaecological procedures were forced to wait much longer. And although in theory termination of pregnancy is available on the NHS, in practice, around half of the women seeking termination of their pregnancy have had to pay for it albeit sometimes at clinics run by charitable organizations.[19] In 1979 the Royal Commission on the National Health Service concluded that only two functions carried out by the private medical sector had an impact on the NHS: abortions and the care of the chronically sick. In 1986, 19 per cent – by far the largest component – of the estimated total caseload of non-NHS hospitals in England and Wales, was abortion.[20]

In 1931, the Ministry of Health issued Memorandum 153/MCW, which conferred on all local health authorities the permissive power to provide birth control advice to married women for whom a further pregnancy would be detrimental to health. At first sight, this development seems to represent a progressive development: the direct involvement by the government in fertility control. However, the ministerial guidelines did not compel local authorities to comply but left it up to local councillors' decision. During the interwar period, municipal and national politics were not wholly assimilated into one another; indeed, in most respects, local politics had a life of their own.[21] In effect, this strategy enabled national government to divorce itself from provision of birth control services; by insisting that monies for them had to be raised from domestic rates, it thereby made them the responsibility of local politicians. Urged on by the birth control lobby, about half of all local authorities took advantage of their power. In 1936, 173 out of 423 local authorities had taken some action on birth control. By 1938, the number had increased to 247 out of 409.[22] And in 1952, the proportion was roughly the same.[23]

Both Conservative and Labour governments succumbed unwillingly to pressure from the antinatalist 'population explosion' lobby which reached the zenith of its influence in the late 1960s and early 1970s. In 1967, the NHS (Family Planning) Act empowered local authorities to provide advice on family planning without regard for marital status, on social as well as medical grounds.

In 1974, the government agreed reluctantly to take over the clinics run by voluntary organizations which, when combined with the local authority clinics, established a national family planning service within the newly reorganized NHS in 1974.[24] Since they were made the responsibility of the NHS, family planning clinics have been underresourced; indeed, the service is slowly being whittled away, because without the protection of the Minister of Health, it is a vulnerable soft target for saving money. As a result, women's access to clinics is being restricted.[25] Increasingly, they are being forced to turn to their GPs for contraceptive advice. This is rather an ironic turn of events. GPs' interpretation of their role as family doctors puts them amongst the staunchest and most persistent opponents of birth control for most of this century. When asked to provide contraceptives to their patients in the 1970s, many objected on the grounds that such activity reduced their professional status to that of a barber or retailer of rubber goods. None the less, when the government agreed to pay them for it, almost all GPs declared themselves willing to prescribe contraceptives.[26] Although GPs are paid out of the NHS budget, they are independent contractors, small businessmen offering a professional service; it is their conscience and enthusiasm and not the Minister of Health that determines the quality of the family planning service provided in Britain.[27]

There are many different types of interest groups. Clearly, a government is one, although in a democracy, it purports to serve the nation, and not the sectional interests of the political party it represents. Interest groups exist within institutions, where they compete with each other in order to gain influence and self-promotion. More typical though are the interest groups which operate outside of institutions, challenging their authority. Other interest groups are established in order to offer a service to the public which local or national government fails to provide. In Britain, voluntary organizations fill in gaps left by the state; provision of childcare and help for the elderly are good examples. Some services which enable women to manage their fertility appear to occupy a similar niche. However, a complex relationship connects these service organizations and national government.[28] In order to escape prosecution, organizations that set out to offer services to the public, especially medical ones, have to negotiate with regulatory bodies set up by the state. In effect, financial and legal requirements mean that activities conducted outside of the government's purview are still regulated by it and hence can never claim to be truly independent of it.

My argument is that by permitting a new service to be offered to the public, a government effectively devolves its responsibility for it.[29] Britain has a long tradition of voluntary bodies undertaking work which political expediency prevents government from doing itself. A good example is provided by birth control clinics that were opened up by individuals like Marie Stopes in the 1920s. How did they escape the threat of criminal prosecution which for decades had dogged neo-Malthusians? The pronounced pronatalism of the first 20 years of the century was overturned in the 1920s as unemployment crept up and political unrest grew. In this unsettled climate, Malthusianism gained cross-party support. However, national political parties refused to commit public money to the provision of birth control advice for fear of jeopardizing electoral support.[30] Instead by doing little to prevent voluntary organizations and local authorities from offering birth control advice to women under certain specified circumstances, the Ministry of Health tacitly condoned antinatalism without putting votes at risk.[31]

British governments do take pro- or antinatalist positions. For electoral and ideological reasons, however, governments find it expedient to call population policies relating to fertility 'health' care, as this rubric glosses them with an altogether different, seemingly benevolent, intention.[32] This shift in nomenclature is a sleight of hand which enables a government to distance itself from politically sensitive areas of medical practice. In the case of abortion, distance has been maintained through the creation of conditions within the NHS which promote and sustain the private medical sector; in the case of birth control, by making women dependent in the first instance on the enthusiasm of local authorities and voluntary organizations such as the Family Planning Association (FPA), and then, from the 1970s onwards, on their GP, an independent contractor. A similar absence of direct intervention has obtained for infertility treatments which, as the chequered history of artificial insemination using donated semen attests, can arouse more public furore than have abortion and contraception.[33] In the case of infertility treatment, distance has been maintained by sustaining and even encouraging private practice. The private medical sector currently caters for a larger proportion of patients undergoing assisted reproduction than for any other elective surgical procedure – three out of 20 people who underwent elective surgery in England and

Wales in 1986, and about 19 out of 20 women who underwent IVF and GIFT.[34] Sustaining private practice in infertility has proved easy, because of its significance to gynaecology.

The economic significance of gynaecological operations

Since the 1930s, medical practitioners have recommended that infertile patients should be seen in a dedicated infertility clinic where the full range of specialist help – gynaecology, endocrinology, urology and laboratory staff – work together as a team and thereby offer a 'state of the art' coordinated service to both male and female patients.[35] The advantages to patients attending dedicated infertility clinics are considerable: there is a greater chance that unnecessary operations are avoided, harmful treatments will not be offered and better results – meaning the birth of a healthy baby – are effected. Nevertheless, most infertility is treated by gynaecologists who see involuntarily childless women and men alongside those seeking termination of pregnancy or who are suffering from problems of menstruation and the menopause. A survey carried out in 1985 by David Mathieson for Frank Dobson, then Labour shadow health minister, found that barely one-third of District Health Authorities in England and Wales had a dedicated infertility clinic.[36] And in Scotland the position is even worse.[37] The situation had not improved by 1990 when Harriet Harman, Dobson's successor, repeated the survey.[38]

Given that men do play a large part in reproduction, why do gynaecologists still monopolise the management of infertility? It is true that when compared to other developed countries, England and Wales are poorly served by specialist urologists, and that few of them are interested in male infertility.[39] Treating male infertility involves engaging with male sexuality, a territory few British (male) scientists and doctors are happy to explore. In the early part of this century, there were good economic reasons for not straying into this territory: urologists won respectability by disassociating their practice from that of quacks – their competitors – who offered nostrums that they claimed would enhance male potency and through it, male fertility.[40] In their promotional literature, quacks cited medical texts of the late nineteenth and early twentieth century which claimed that *potentia coeundi* (sexual potency) meant *potentia generandi* (power to procreate).

No doubt the reluctance of urologists to engage with male fertility explains partially the absence of teamwork in infertility clinics today. But I suggest that the main reason why dedicated infertility clinics – which are best-suited to the conditions found in a large NHS hospital – are a rarity is that their institution depends on the enthusiasm of individual specialists who alone have the authority to persuade medical colleagues and convince administrative and nursing staff of the need to reorganize existing facilities. In the past, some consultant gynaecologists exploited their freedom of action to prevent the development of services relating to fertility control; for example, in the West Midlands, it is almost impossible for women to obtain an abortion on the NHS because devout catholic consultants have appointed as many fellow believers to posts in their region as they could.[41] Similarly, the rapid growth of clinics offering IVF within NHS premises but not funded by the service, is proof of the ability of gynaecologists to move institutional and financial mountains when they want to.

Until recently, gynaecologists working within the NHS had little incentive to offer a well-organized service to infertile patients; women and men dissatisfied with NHS treatment could be channelled into private practice. The contrast between the two sectors is marked. A letter in *Issue*, the journal of the National Association of the Childless, gave readers the following advice: 'go without holidays etc. and seek treatment in a reputable [private] clinic rather than spend frustrating months at a National Health clinic'.[42]

Throughout the twentieth century, the investigation and treatment of infertility has been an important source of income for gynaecologists. As I will show, supported by their professional body, the Royal College of Obstetricians and Gynaecologists, gynaecologists have resisted any attempt to make more widely available free, modern treatment. The story of gynaecologists' campaigns to safeguard their incomes derived from infertility treatment begins in the 1930s when a number of developments combined to challenge the status quo.

Before the introduction of the NHS, unlike male workers, most women who were not pregnant or nursing a young baby and who wanted medical treatment had to pay for it. We know from the campaigns waged to remedy this discriminatory state of affairs the price paid by poorer women – both physically and financially.[43] Many women suffered from minor gynaecological problems. Indeed, in the 1930s their prevalence led some local authorities to argue that the legislation that introduced maternal and child welfare clinics should be extended to cover the provision of gynaecological treatment to these women.[44] A combination of cost, inaccessibility and embarrassment may explain why, before the NHS, so few poor, involuntarily childless women consulted a GP or a hospital outpatient clinic. A survey carried out in the mid 1940s by the Royal College of Obstetricians and Gynaecologists on behalf of the Royal Commission on Population, found that only 34 out of the 176 childless women of completed fertility married between 1920 and 1924 – just under one in five – had consulted a doctor about their infertility.[45] Significantly, poorer women were overrepresented in the sample.

Workers in the clinics that had been set up from the 1920s onwards by birth control activists to help women not to have children were surprised by the number of women who sought their help to have a child.[46] Some of the clinics,

especially those that were more like an out-patient gynaecological dispensary than a birth control clinic, began to give
infertile women advice or refer them for medical help
elsewhere.[47] The National Birth Control Association,
founded in 1930 to coordinate the work of the existing birth
control organizations (except those run by Marie Stopes),
changed its name in 1939 to the Family Planning Association
(FPA). The new name reflects the change in its aims; from
helping poorer women not to have children to promoting
planned and happy working-class families by offering advice
on birth control, treatment for involuntary sterility and
counselling for difficulties with the marriage relationship.[48]

Another reason why the FPA widened its objectives was
that, during the 1930s the threat of depopulation made the
promotion of birth control seem unpatriotic. The increasingly tense international climate and the fascists' enthusiasm
for boosting the size and altering the composition of their
populations, brought about a resurgence of pronatalism in
England. Unfortunately, as the unemployment rate reached
its zenith, the birth rate of all social classes fell to its nadir.
Some people felt that a smaller population was a good thing;
there would be fewer people competing for jobs. Others,
especially members of the Eugenics Society, believed that
Britain desperately needed more babies if it was to continue
as a world power. The FPA had close links with and was
partially supported by the Eugenics Society, which, through
its research into population policies in Europe, was aware
that in 1926 Mussolini had introduced a comprehensive
pronatalist programme and that in 1933 Nazi Germany had
followed suit in order to boost the Aryan birth rate. Both
programmes included medical treatment for sterility.
Eugenicists' ideas underwent a reversal: to save Britain and
the Empire, they were prepared to persuade women of the
most numerous section of the population – the working class
– to have more babies.

The FPA's plans to promote the treatment of infertility
were not advanced formally until some four years later

when, in March 1943, an ad hoc committee on subfertility was set up. Nevertheless, some birth control clinics began to treat sterility. For example, in 1941, 57 women sought advice at the North Kensington Women's Welfare Centre because they wanted children and the Centre began to consider opening a special session for the treatment of sterility.[49] The membership of the FPA's ad hoc committee included leading London-based male gynaecologists and female medical practitioners who had a special interest in both birth control and sterility. Their plan was to introduce a scheme that would show up the shortcomings of existing services. As Margaret Jackson, a committee member, put it:

> Family Planning Association clinics have a definite role to fill; by creating a demand for good thorough work they may galvanize the hospitals into more effective action, and they can act as sorting and coordinating centres and as sources of material for research . . . what general hospital has such easy access to large groups of subfertile patients as are available at FPA clinics to act as controls of the many difficult problems confronting those who attempt to investigate, diagnose and treat subfertility?[50]

The plan was to introduce 'Motherhood' sessions in their clinics where women whose family income did not exceed £5 a week could obtain treatment for a small fee. And because only two or three doctors in England were believed to be competent in seminological analysis, the FPA decided to establish its own centre in London where semen and post-coital tests could be carried out for the clinics' patients as well as those of other doctors; payment would be according to means.[51]

The FPA's proposals met with a hostile response from both GPs and the Royal College of Obstetricians and Gynaecologists. GPs claimed that, as family doctors, they were most suited to deal with and had the greatest understanding of patients' private and intimate problems like involuntary childlessness. The FPA's clinics were impersonal and treated women as just another number. A GP offered patients the best of both worlds: he could use his personal relationship to tackle any emotional difficulties and, by referral to a gynaecologist, offered patients access to up-to-date tests and treatments.[52] Despite these protestations, it is clear that some GPs had little interest in sterility and sent their patients away without ordering tests or treatment. Indeed, many of the women who sought help from infertility clinics learnt about them from articles in newspapers and magazines and not from their GPs.[53]

The RCOG's stated objection was that the women doctors who staffed the FPA's clinics did not have sufficient expertise to carry out tests and advise on treatments. Sterility was a complex condition which demanded the expertise that only a leading consultant possessed. While they acknowledged that there was a lack of modern facilities for the treatment of sterility, their solution was to work with the Medical Research Council (MRC) on improving laboratory practices and to encourage more teaching hospitals to set up specialist clinics.[54] It is not clear what gynaecologists expected involuntarily childless women to do meanwhile unless they meant them to seek private medical care. For in the 1940s, in England and Wales, only ten hospitals (five of them in London) had special clinics dedicated to the treatment of sterility: the other five were in Aylesbury, Barrow-in-Furness, Colchester, Oxford and Plymouth.[55] Men were very poorly served: 12 of the 27 London hospitals and 49 of the 94 provincial hospitals had no facilities for investigating male fertility. There were six private specialists treating sterility in London, only two of whom saw men.[56] A few hospitals had considered setting up infertility clinics, encouraged perhaps by the pronatalist climate of the 1930s, but war had disrupted their plans.[57]

Before and during the war, several local authorities had contacted the Ministry of Health to find out whether the legislation that enabled them to give free medical advice to pregnant and nursing mothers could be extended to cover women who wanted to have children.[58] The Ministry looked into the regulations covering maternal and child welfare services and contacted both the Royal College of Obstetricians and Gynaecologists and the MRC for guidance. The MRC and the RCOG set up a Committee on Human Fertility which held its first meeting in January 1944.[59] The committee was taken over and enlarged by the Royal Commission on Population where it was renamed The Biological and Medical Committee.

The Royal Commission, which had been set up in response to the pronatalist anxieties of the 1930s, took up the issue of involuntary childlessness in a comprehensive way. Its Report published in 1949 recommended that the newly formed NHS should set up family planning clinics where advice on marriage difficulties, birth control and sterility would be provided. Unfortunately, no notice was taken of any of the Commission's recommendations. With the exception of one question to the Chancellor of the Exchequer which ascertained that implementing its recommendations would cost the taxpayer £200 million, the Report was never discussed in Parliament. No one in the cabinet was willing to champion such a politically sensitive cause.[60]

In 1947, the FPA reached a formal agreement with the British Medical Association about where and what type of Motherhood clinic they could set up.[61] In practice, opposition of GPs and gynaecologists as well as reluctance of some of the women doctors who worked in the FPA's clinics and who were also employed as medical assistants in nearby hospitals, meant that the type of service offered was determined by local conditions. Where they met with little opposition – indicating that there was no competition – the FPA set up Motherhood sessions staffed either by a woman gynaecologist who carried out the full range of tests, or by another clinic doctor who did some preliminary work but referred patients to the nearest specialist for more technically demanding tests and treatments.[62] In other clinics, infertile women were seen alongside those seeking advice on how not to have a baby. The clinic doctor would offer some preliminary guidance and refer the woman to a local gynaecologist. The FPA's ad hoc committee also encouraged the development of a consensus on interpreting infertility investigations, especially semen tests, which were notoriously unreliable. It held several annual conferences where papers on research into the physiology of reproduction and new types of treatments were read and discussed. The organization of these conferences was taken over in 1950 by the newly formed Society for the Study of Fertility.

Although the introduction of the NHS made free gynaecological treatment available to all women, nothing was done to improve the provision of infertility services. In 1950 the Royal College of Obstetricians and Gynaecologists passed a resolution that infertility should be a function of all gynaecological clinics and not just special infertility clinics.[63] The Ministry of Health continued to distance itself from the service; in 1964, it admitted that not one circular had been sent to hospitals on the organization of infertility services.[64]

Income from private practice declined in the early days of the NHS and gynaecologists became more dependent on their salaries. The RCOG continued its opposition to the FPA's Motherhood clinics.[65] But the FPA persisted in its challenge to private practice: in 1950, seven of its clinics held Motherhood sessions,[66] in 1957, 12,[67] in 1960, 28[68] and in 1965, 48.[69] And as its policy was to concentrate on those parts of the country where NHS facilities were inadequate, this growth in numbers reflects a lack of specialist facilities for the treatment of infertility within the NHS. Unfortunately, the FPA's infertility clinics virtually disappeared when they were taken over by the NHS in 1974.

Gynaecological balance sheets and the new reproductive technologies

Shunned by the London medical establishment and denied research funds, during the 1970s Patrick Steptoe and Robert Edwards developed the technique of *in vitro* fertilization in the tiny, yet cosy-sounding, Kershaw Cottage Hospital, near Oldham, Lancashire.[70] It was only after the birth of the first 'test tube' baby in 1978 which coincided with Steptoe's retirement from his NHS appointment, that the two pioneers set up Bourn Hall, a private IVF clinic, which was opened in 1980.[71] Seven years later, reflecting the speed with which IVF has transformed the players in the market for infertility treatment, Bourn Hall was sold to Ares-Serono, a multi-national company and the world's major supplier of infertility drugs.[72] The following year, Bourn Hall merged with the Hallam Centre, a Harley Street private infertility clinic, to form Bourn–Hallam; Ares-Serono now boasts that it owns the largest IVF centre in the world, carrying out 2,500 IVF and GIFT cycles a year as well as a large number of frozen embryo replacement cycles, artificial insemination, surrogacy and other infertility treatments.[73]

Although a great deal of attention has been given to the profit and loss accounts of IVF centres, one of the least-discussed aspects of the new reproductive technologies is their impact on the balance sheet and working capital of gynaecological practice in Britain. In the past, the treatment of infertility rarely required the sophisticated support services that are demanded by IVF. All that was needed to carry out a post-coital test – once the mainstay of infertility investigations – was a couch, a speculum, a syringe and a microscope. Harley Street consultants could send patients to one of the private pathology laboratories for semen and blood tests. In contrast, setting up an IVF clinic requires a large capital investment. In 1988, an investment of £550,000 was needed in order to set up a clinic with the facilities to offer IVF to 400 women each year.[74] In the same year, a group of enterprising gynaecologists from the St James's Hospital, Leeds (Jimmy's), attempted to raise £1m capital from the stock market in order to set up a private IVF clinic.

In the early days of the NHS, consultants were encouraged to undertake private practice within its hospitals and discouraged from sending patients to small, unsuitable private nursing homes dotted around the country.[75] However, in 1976, the Labour government of Harold Wilson abolished NHS 'pay beds' and removed other advantages of paying for treatment in NHS hospitals. Private and NHS patients were given the same status on waiting lists and parity of access to NHS diagnostic and other services. Labour's attack on private practice was bitterly resented and proved counter-productive: the 'pay-beds' dispute gave consultants a greater incentive to work in the private sector which offered them income, autonomy and work in congenial surroundings. The Conservative government that was returned in 1979 was committed to encouraging private medicine and, in 1980, passed three measures that reintroduced private practice into the NHS. The Health Services Act, 1980, reduced restrictions on private medicine in the NHS, legalized lotteries and permitted health authorities to engage in voluntary fund-raising; a voluntary code of practice was drawn up designed to safeguard NHS facilities from abuse by private patients but the mechanism for monitoring has proved low-key; NHS consultants' contracts were altered so that they could undertake significantly more private practice without forfeiting their positions and privileges in the NHS.[76] Since then, patients and health authorities have begun to look outside of the public sector for health care resources.

The incorporation of IVF into the clinical repertoire coincided with the Conservative government's health care policy of establishing a mixed economy and encouraging competition in health care. And the special position of infertility within the NHS made it uniquely well equipped to take advantage of the new political climate. Indeed, IVF has put gynaecology in the vanguard of the privatization of the NHS. Gynaecologists working within the NHS have demonstrated considerable business flair. By taking full advantage of their new ability to raise funds, they have developed quasi-private clinics using staff, equipment and drugs paid for by a mixture of the NHS, research and drug company monies, and charges to patients. In some hospitals, patients are asked to make a 'voluntary' contribution; in others, the patients' support group raises money to buy equipment. So valuable is the contribution to capital costs of support groups, that one consultant advised his colleagues to set one up before opening a clinic.[77] Some consultants operate a 'Robin Hood' system: 'robbing' better-off patients in order to provide free treatment for people who might otherwise go without. The most inventive scheme was developed by the Fazakerley Hospital, Liverpool, where an incentive scheme is run in conjunction with a 'Robin Hood' system. People on the incentive scheme who raise funds for the unit get credits which count towards the cost of their treatment: £1,200 raised qualifies a patient for a free treatment cycle.[78]

By attaching an IVF clinic on to existing NHS facilities, gynaecologists avoid having to find the large start-up capital costs of an independent unit. Another strategy is to combine an NHS centre with one in a private clinic nearby.[79] Most of these innovative schemes have been developed by relatively small units where the chances of women becoming pregnant are slight. Admittedly, the greatest number of IVF treatment cycles are carried out in the wholly private medical sector. Nevertheless, the very existence of these quasi-private clinics within NHS hospitals serves an important ideological purpose: they are both an emblem of the new political economy of health care and a reminder of the government's reluctance to support openly a medical service involved in the management of women's fertility.

Conclusion

One of the recommendations of the Warnock Report on human fertilization and embryology in 1984 was that national guidelines on the organization of services for the treatment of infertility should be established.[80] True to form, this advice went unheeded; instead, the Conservative government focused on the aspect of the new reproductive technologies that posed the greatest threat to its parliamentary majority: the traffic in and manipulation of human gametes and embryos. In order to safeguard the moral future of human gametes and embryos, the Human Fertilization and Embryology Act, 1990 – the first piece of legislation relating to women's fertility introduced by a British government – is denying access to infertility treatment to women deemed 'unsuitable' as mothers. And as a result of the government's reorganization of the NHS and the creation of an 'internal market', the cash nexus is being strengthened; faced with the need to ration health care, many health authorities are excluding from their shopping lists IVF and other infertility treatments. Now more than ever before, money and social status are determining who can get treatment for infertility in Britain.

Notes

I should like to thank Frances Price and Meg Stacey for their helpful comments on this chapter. I am grateful to the Economic and Social Research Council for their support of my doctoral thesis on which parts of this chapter are based. I would like to record my thanks to The Wellcome Trust for a Fellowship which enabled me to write this chapter.

1 Interim Licensing Authority (1991) *The Sixth Report of the Interim Licensing Authority for Human in Vitro Fertilisation and Embryology*, London, Interim Licensing Authority: 12. The Authority was set up in 1985 by the Medical Research Council and the Royal College of Obstetricians and Gynaecologists to regulate IVF clinics and research on human embryos. The Authority was seen as a temporary measure, its existence would cease when a statutory authority was established by

the government. At first, it called itself a 'Voluntary' authority; in 1989, it changed its name to 'Interim'. On 1 August 1991, the Authority was replaced by the Human Fertilization and Embryology Authority. The system of regulation set up in Britain is unique; in each country where IVF is offered, regulation and provision is determined by an admixture of history, the political economy of medicine and political organization. For a suggestive catalogue of international regulation of research on the treatment with human embryos, see Jennifer Gunning (1990) *Human IVF, Embryo Research, Fetal Tissue for Research and Treatment, and Abortion: International Information*, London, HMSO.

2 Marsden Wagner and Patricia St Clair (1989) 'Are in-vitro fertilisation and embryo transfer of benefit to all?' *Lancet*, 28 October: 1027–30.

3 A good example is an article published in The *Guardian* newspaper on the birth of the first baby born as result of the technique of pre-uterine self-incubation. Headed 'New hope for the infertile', the article does not mention efficacy or safety; instead, it emphasizes the cheapness of this technique compared to that of other approaches to IVF. Alan Dunn (1989) 'Birth brings new hope to the infertile', *Guardian*, 30 September: 6.

4 J. Watson (1989) 'Clinic urged to scrap offer of test-tube babies on credit', *Scotland on Sunday*, 12 November.

5 (1989) 'Wife stole for test tube op', *Mirror*, 12 May.

6 Before the ILA's sixth report, published in 1991, the reasons why some centres succeeded in making a higher than average proportion of women pregnant whereas others had a very low success rate, were not made explicit. In 1989, the average live-birth rate per treatment cycle was 11.1 per cent; however, five clinics achieved less than a 6 per cent live-birth rate per treatment cycle. According to the ILA, there were good clinical reasons for these lower success rates; for example, preparedness to treat older women and couples with so-called 'male factor infertility' (ILA (1991) *The Sixth Report*: 14–15). There is no doubt though that other clinics lack the necessary expertise. According to the ILA: 'there is a definite learning curve and the best results are obtained from those centres with well-qualified and established teams' (ILA (1991) *The Sixth Report*: 5). There is no recognized training course for embryologists, who vary according to background and training.

7 ILA (1990) *The Fifth Report of the Interim Licensing Authority for Human in Vitro Fertilisation and Embryology,* London, ILA: 2.

8 For a discussion of the language of consumerism in health care, see Naomi Pfeffer and Anna Coote (1991) *Is Quality Good for you? A Critical Review of Quality Assurance in welfare services,* London,

Institute for Public Policy Research: 15–19.
9 Naomi Pfeffer (1985) 'Not so new technology: infertility and feminism', *Trouble and Strife*, 5: 46–50.
10 For a good discussion of whether the NHS should offer IVF, see H. Page (1989) 'Economic appraisal of in vitro fertilization: discussion paper', *Journal of the Royal Society of Medicine*, 88: 99–102.
11 Ornella Moscucci draws attention to the importance of economic considerations to the development of gynaecology since its inception as a speciality. See O. Moscucci (1990) *The Science of Gynaecology. Gynaecology and Gender in England, 1800–1929*, Cambridge, Cambridge University Press.
12 For a discussion of issues around private medical care in Britain, see D.A. Horne (1986) 'Public policy making and private medical care in the United Kingdom since 1948', unpublished PhD thesis, University of Bath; B. Griffith, S. Iliffe and G. Rayner (1987) *Banking on Sickness*, London, Lawrence and Wishart; J. Higgins (1988) *The Business of Medicine. Private Health Care in Britain*, Basingstoke, Macmillan; J. Busfield (1990) 'Sectoral divisions in consumption: the case of medical care', *Sociology*, 24, 1: 77–96. For a discussion of the reasons why British women have hysterectomies, see Angela Coulter and Klim McPherson (1986) 'The hysterectomy debate', *Quarterly Journal of Social Affairs*, 2: 379–96.
13 Gunning, *Human IVF*: 5.
14 Paolo De Sandre (1978) 'The influence of governments', in Council of Europe (ed.), *Population Decline in Europe. Implications of a Declining or Stationary Population*, London, Edward Arnold: 145–70.
15 See J. Weeks (1981) *Sex, Politics and Society*, London, Longman.
16 For an excellent discussion of the state and population policies, see D. Riley (1981) 'Feminist thought and reproductive control: the state and "the right to choose"', in The Cambridge Women's Studies Group (eds), *Women in Society*, London, Virago: 185–200.
17 In Britain today, only the Green Party admits openly to having a policy on the growth of population in Britain. I asked the Conservative Party's Central Office if the Party had a policy on population. Although the Party takes a firm line on immigration, my question was not understood; instead, they offered to send me statistics on population size, etc. The Labour Party drew my attention to the sections of its health policy relating to contraception, abortion and infertility treatment. See Naomi Pfeffer (1990) 'Fertility control: health or population policy?', *Critical Public Health*, 2: 19–21.
18 See histories of birth control and abortion: B. Brookes (1988) *Abortion in England 1900–67*, London, Croom Helm; D. Marsh and J. Chambers (1981) *Abortion Politics*, London, Junction Books; Robert

Dowse and J. Peel (1965) 'The politics of birth control', *Political Studies*, 13: 179–97; A. Leathard (1980) *The Fight for Family Planning*, London, Macmillan; R. Soloway (1982) *Birth Control and the Population Question*, Chapel Hill, The University of North Carolina.

19 For example, in Bristol, the Abortion Act increased the waiting list for inpatient gynaecological treatment at NHS hospitals from 240 patients in 1964 to 708 in 1971. See A.H. John and B. Hackman (1972) 'Effects of legal abortion on gynaecology', *British Medical Journal*, ii: 99–102.

20 J.P. Nicholl, N.R. Beeby, B.T. Williams (1989) 'Comparison of the activity of short stay independent hospitals in England and Wales, 1981 and 1986', *British Medical Journal*, i: 239–42. Data are not available on the proportion abortions represent to the work of NHS hospitals.

21 J. Gyford (1985) 'The politicization of local government', in M. Loughlin, M. Gelfand and K. Young (eds), *Half a Century of Municipal Decline, 1935–85*, London, George Allen & Unwin: 82–3.

22 PRO MH 52/198B.

23 Family Planning Committee of the Medical Women's Federation (1952) 'Memorandum on family planning, with particular reference to contraception', *British Medical Journal*, i: 595–7.

24 For a discussion of the conflict between the government and antinatalist interests in the early 1970s, see D. McKie (1973) 'Family planning and the NHS', *Lancet*, i: 715.

25 See A. Leathard (1985) *District Health Authority Family Planning Services in England and Wales*, London, Family Planning Association.

26 In the first half of the 1970s, on behalf of GPs, the British Medical Association fought hard and long over this issue. The *British Medical Journal* of that period contains numerous articles and letters that record their campaign.

27 Hospital and GP services are organized separately within the NHS. The Ministry of Health has a greater influence on services provided by hospitals than by GPs.

28 Hindess draws attention to the complex conditions in which political concerns and interests are formed and the ways in which their invocation may play a role in political life. B. Hindess (1986) '"Interests" in political analysis', in J. Law (ed.), *Power, Action and Belief*, London, Routledge & Kegan Paul: 112–31.

29 See B. Barnes (1986) 'On authority and its relationship to power', in J. Law (ed.), *Power, Action and Belief*, London, Routledge & Kegan Paul: 180–195.

30 R.E. Dowse and J. Peel (1965) 'The politics of birth control', *Political Studies*, 13: 179–97.

31 Historians of the birth control movement have tended to portray

developments such as this as a successful battle in the campaign waged by the forces of enlightenment against those of reaction. They do this by deploying military metaphors; Leathard's book is called *The Fight for Family Planning*; the final chapter of Soloway's *Birth Control and the Population Question*, is called 'The walls of the citadel fall'. I suggest that the politics of fertility control in Britain are more complex than these historians suggest.

32 I was alerted to the political significance of a distinction between 'population' and 'health' by the discovery that after the oil crisis of the 1970s, governments of developing countries which expelled international agencies promoting birth control in order to keep down their population growth, then introduced similar programmes under the rubric of 'health'.

33 See Naomi Pfeffer (1987) 'Artificial insemination, *in vitro* fertilisation and the stigma of infertility', in M. Stanworth (ed.), *Reproductive Technologies*, Cambridge, Polity Press: 81–97.

34 J.P. Nicholl, N.R. Beeby, B.T. Williams (1989) 'Role of the private sector in elective surgery in England and Wales, 1986', *British Medical Journal*, 298: 243–7.

35 The American gynaecologist Samuel Meaker, was the first to organize infertility clinics on these lines. His methods were widely publicized in England during the 1930s, and became the benchmark of good practice. See for example CMAC SA/EUG/N 52.

36 David Mathieson (1986) *Infertility Services in the NHS; What's Going On? A Report Prepared for Frank Dobson MP*, London, House of Commons: 8.

37 National Association for the Childless Scotland (1989) *The Organisation and Management of Infertility*, NAC Scotland.

38 H. Harman (1990) *Trying for a Baby. A Report on the Inadequacy of NHS Infertility Service*, London, House of Commons.

39 Royal College of Surgeons of England (1986) *Commission on the Provision of Surgical Services. General Surgical Manpower Within the United Kingdom*, London, Royal College of Surgeons.

40 For an entertaining account of doctors' reluctance to engage with problems of male sexuality, see Lesley Hall (1991) *Hidden Anxieties. Male Sexuality, 1900–1950*, Cambridge, Polity Press.

41 British Pregnancy Advisory Services (BPAS), a charity, was set up in order to provide services for women seeking termination of pregnancy in the West Midlands.

42 J. & C. Townsend (1987) 'Wasted years', *Issue*, 5: 24.

43 See for example, M. Spring Rice (1981) *Working-class Wives*, London, Virago.

44 PRO MH 52 198/B and PRO MH 55/1503.

45 E. Lewis-Faning (1949) *Report on an Inquiry into Family Limitation and its Influence on Human Fertility During the Past 50 Years*, London, HMSO: 90–1.
46 G. Cox and M. Jackson (1934) 'Birth control clinics and cases of sterility', *British Medical Journal*, i: 174; Marie Stopes (1943) 'Sterility and contraception', *British Medical Journal*, ii: 256.
47 PRO MH 52/198B; CMAC SA/FPA NK/90.
48 CMAC SA/FPA A5/1081.
49 PRO MH 55/1503.
50 M. Jackson (1943) 'Contraception and sterility', *Lancet*, ii: 691.
51 CMAC SA/FPA A5/102 and SA/FPA A5/103.
52 The records of the North Kensington Women's Welfare Centre, show that many women sought their advice on sterility because their GP was not interested in it. CMAC SA/FPA NK/90.
53 A letter from Medical Officer, Subfertility clinic (1950) 'Fertility and family planning', *Lancet*, i: 180.
54 PRO MH 58/399. From the late 1930s onwards, the RCOG was asked to support a number of endeavours to make treatment of sterility available to poorer women. Their response was always the same: they refused to be associated with these ventures and told their advocates to advise women to consult a doctor. See for example RCOG A3/4.
55 PRO RG 24/5.
56 CMAC SA/FPA A3/20.
57 RCOG D7/3.
58 PRO MH 58/399.
59 MRC 2526.
60 PRO CAB 124/1037.
61 CMAC SA/FPA A3/23.
62 Motherhood clinics offered advice, a physical examination, endometrial biopsy, salpingogram and tubal insufflation. Semen and post-coital tests were carried out at the FPA's pathological centre in London.
63 RCOG A3/7; RCOG A2/5 and Council Minute Book 6.
64 CMAC SA/FPA A3/23.
65 RCOG Council Minute Book 6: 17 July 1951.
66 CMAC SA/FPA A3/27.
67 CMAC SA/FPA A3/26.
68 CMAC SA/FPA A5/64.
69 CMAC SA/FPA A5/62.
70 A. Veitch (1988) 'A man who made thousands of babies', *Guardian*, 23 March: 19.
71 See Robert Edwards and Patrick Steptoe (1981) *A Matter of Life. The Sensational Story of the World's First Test-tube Baby*, London, Sphere Books. Bourn Hall was chosen because it was close to the Cambridge

laboratories of Edwards. I have been unable to ascertain who provided Steptoe and Edwards with the necessary capital.

72 Ares-Serono is a medium-sized international drug company with executive headquarters in Geneva, Switzerland. The company is the world's leading producer of fertility drugs which, in 1988 comprised 84 per cent of its turnover of $420.3 m.

73 Peter R. Brinsden (n.d.) *Infertility and IVF. Patient Information Booklet*, Cambridge, Bourn Hall.

74 Professor Robert Winston, a leading infertility specialist, provided these figures at the annual general meeting of the National Association for the Childless, September 1988.

75 Higgins, *The Business of Medicine*: 18. Both GPs and gynaecologists used cottage hospitals and private nursing homes for investigations and treatment of infertility. Many of them were closed in the 1980s which meant that GPs were forced out of infertility work and gynaecologists had to find alternative facilities.

76 Higgins, *The Business of Medicine*: 85–6.

77 John Parson (1987) 'Funding an assisted conception unit in an NHS hospital', *Conceive*, 7.

78 I am indebted to Mary-Claire Mason for this information.

79 For example, St Bartholomew's Hospital, London, (Barts), a prestigious teaching hospital, has a joint operation with the AMI Portland Clinic, a private hospital for women specializing in gynaecology and obstetrics. The Portland supports Barts by paying part of the salary of a consultant gynaecologist, and for two embryologists, who work at both units.

80 M. Warnock (1985) *A Question of Life*, Oxford, Blackwells: 14.

4

Making sense of missed conceptions: anthropological perspectives on unexplained infertility

SARAH FRANKLIN

Explanations of conception and procreation have long been of intrinsic interest to anthropology (see Montagu, 1937). The discipline itself was founded amidst debates concerning the negotiation of parenthood and procreation, kinship reckonings and conception stories. Central to these debates has been the issue of the relationship between the so-called 'natural facts' of human reproduction and the various cultural elaborations brought to bear on what is considered to be its objective, biogenetic basis.

The classic anthropological controversy known as the 'virgin birth' debates proceeded from the discovery of cultures which do not believe in the biological model of conception (see Delaney, 1986). When Malinowski visited the Trobriand islands of Melanesia, he tried hard to convince his informants of their oversight in thinking that a male contribution was unnecessary to the production of a pregnancy. Was it not true, he insisted, that intercourse is necessary for conception to occur? His informants remained firm. Why, they replied, if there is a causal relationship between intercourse and pregnancy, do so many young girls who have intercourse not become pregnant (Malinowski, 1925)? Children, they argued, result from the return of an ancestor through the body of a woman. Hence, the matrilineage is preserved, as a woman's ancestors return through her to produce offspring. Hence, the central mechanism of Trobriand social organization, the matrilineal clan, through which new Trobrianders come into being and acquire a specific identity and meaningful kinship ties and obligations (see Malinowski, 1916, 1929; Weiner, 1976, 1988).

Anthropologists have offered many explanations of peoples, such as the Trobrianders, who reject biological accounts of conception (Leach, 1966; Spiro, 1968). These range across the entire gamut of anthropological thought, invoking a set of questions about theory, method and cross-cultural comparison which are too numerous to describe here. At the root of this controversy is the assumption that beliefs about parenthood and procreation represent key cultural constructs, the interpretation of which is therefore of critical importance, to anthropologists, as well as the peoples they study.

In contemporary British culture, we are unaccustomed to thinking of our accounts of conception as cultural constructions. On the contrary, we assume the causal relationship between intercourse and pregnancy is a matter of scientific fact. Anglicans may still debate the virgin birth, but such uncertainty is considered to be of a distinctly theological character. In secular life, we are certain about the events which cause pregnancy. Pregnancy is caused by the meeting of the sperm and egg, which fertilize to produce an embryo which develops inside the womb into a child.

However, neither natural science nor natural facts are independent of the cultural context in which they are produced. Like those of other cultures, our conception stories have changed historically, and emerge in the context of specific social formations (see Laqueur, 1986). Moreover, we are currently in the midst of a major elaboration of the biogenetic events involved in reproduction. This is partly due to the emergence of new reproductive technologies which have removed conception from inside the body and made it visible for scientific scrutiny. It is also because of the importance attributed to the events of conception in understanding the mechanisms of genetic inheritance, which are currently receiving an unprecedented degree of scientific attention, as evidenced by major global scientific efforts such as that of mapping the human genome.

While it is seen to be a set of natural facts, we are also familiar with the representation of conception as a narrative (Martin, 1991). In the standard conception narrative, authenticated by biological science, the facts of life unfold along a well-known trajectory. After the sperm are released into the vaginal cavity, they swim into the cervix and up into the uterus and fallopian tubes where they meet the egg, which has come down to meet them from the ovary. When they meet, the sperm and egg merge, at which point fertilization takes place. As the fertilized egg begins to subdivide and develop, it implants itself into the wall of the uterus thus establishing a pregnancy.

This standard conception narrative is more or less how all of us were told about the 'natural facts' connecting intercourse and pregnancy, and accounting for the biological mechanisms of human procreation. Like all narratives, this linear construction of events involves the establishment of a causal sequence from starting point to ending point through which the various components of the narrative are linked. Under most circumstances, this narrative functions adequately as both a representation and an explanation of the causal sequence of events involved in conception. It is, after all, not a very complicated story.

New conception stories

One of the most immediate means of appreciating the changing cultural construction of conception is to consider how this staple narrative is changing. The most important change is that this narrative is becoming much more complex. It is also getting longer, as both the starting points and the ending points of the narrative are extended. It is also becoming less certain, as gaps are opened up in the causal sequence which holds the narrative together. It is becoming less 'natural', as technology increasingly enters into this narrative as an agent in its own right. From the perspective of both social and natural facts, conception stories are becoming more elaborate.

One of the main reasons for these changes in accounts of conception is the growing awareness of the large number of people for whom the standard conception narrative does not function. We are increasingly aware, that is, of the number of people for whom intercourse does not cause pregnancy, whose egg and sperm do not fertilize, whose embryos do not implant, and so forth. These are the couples who are undergoing infertility treatment.

For such couples, and the clinicians who treat them, and the researchers who study them, the standard conception narrative is inadequate. The causal chain established by biological science and assumed as commonsense has broken down. This reveals a very interesting feature of our conception stories. The chain of causality, it is revealed, only functions as a successful explanation system *retrospectively*. It provides a wholly adequate explanation for why conception has occurred *if it has occurred*. In the situation in which the causal factor is present but the hoped-for outcome fails to occur, there is an unexplained event.

The world of achieved conception

Once they are excluded from the standard conception narrative, infertile couples who seek medical assistance come to inhabit a very different world of conception. This might usefully be described as the world of achieved conception. Moving into the world of achieved conception entails a number of significant shifts. From a private and personal matter, conception becomes a public event involving teams of professional experts. From a non-commercial activity, conception takes on a commercial dimension, and the couple become consumers in the marketplace of infertility services on offer. Once taken for granted as a simple natural sequence, conception becomes a technologically assisted achievement. In sum, conception is transformed from a simple narrative into a story that is much more complex, uncertain and mysterious.

Infertility guidebooks, of which there is a rapidly expanding genre, offer a useful introduction to the world of achieved conception, to the new conception narratives emerging out of the context of infertility treatment. The following is a short list of chapter headings from a guidebook of this sort:

How the Ovaries Work
How Men Make Sperm
The Modern Semen Analysis
Mechanical Obstructions
Blocked Ducts and Other Transport Problems
Microsurgery, Lasers and the 21st Century
Miracle Babies
Brave New World

This list, from a book entitled *The Fertility Handbook* (Bellina and Wilson, 1986), provides a useful introduction to the content and parameters of emergent conception stories in the context of *assisted* reproduction. To begin with, the starting point of the conception narrative has been moved back in time to encompass the production of gametes, egg and sperm, not simply their journeys from their point of origin to their eventual rendezvous. Secondly, the topology of achieved conception, heavily indebted to the analogy of plumbing, is defined in terms of the various conduits and passageways which may be obstructed or blocked. Most notably, this world is defined by a particular relationship between modern science and reproductive physiology. It is thanks to modern science we can see, name, understand and control this new domain, and this achievement is seen as a definitively modern one, associated with the advance of scientific progress. Achieved conception foregrounds the enabling potential of technology to overcome 'natural' error. Miracle babies and laser surgery are part of the brave new world of achieved conception in the twenty-first century.

Finally, the world of achieved conception is defined by specific parameters, most notably those of biological science and medical technology. These can be seen to operate discursively, in the Foucauldian sense of 'the delimination of a field of objects, the definition of a legitimate perspective for the agent of knowledge, and the fixing of norms for the elaboration of concepts and theories' (Foucault, 1977: 199). Meaningful information in the context of achieved conception is information which can reveal the biological obstacles to conception, and this information is acquired through technological investigation and monitoring: ultrasound scans, laparoscopy, measurement of hormone levels and so forth. These discursive parameters frame the context within which both infertile couples and clinicians attempt to make sense of missed conceptions.

The world of achieved conception presents not only a changed landscape in the sense of changing natural facts, but a changed landscape of social facts and cultural meanings. It should be remembered that anthropological interest in conception accounts is not merely motivated by a desire to understand the social construction of natural facts. It is also motivated by the assumption that this process of social construction is quite fundamental to a culture's definition of itself. Conception stories not only tell us where we came from – they tell us who we are, how we are related to others, what our kinship obligations are, and how we are situated in patterns of inheritance and descent. They are central to the acquisition of a specific cultural identity, to definitions of sexual difference, personhood, parenthood and procreation. What a culture believes about conception, Malinowski argued, tells you what it believes about everything else. Conception stories are cultural cosmologies in microcosm.

What then are the cultural implications of the changing definition of conception? What are the consequences of this brave new world of achieved conception, miracle babies and state-of-the-art reproductive technologies which are dramatically altering our perception of 'the facts of life'? To answer this question, we are indebted to the experience of those who have inhabited this new frontier and begun to chart its contours. These are the couples who have undergone extensive treatment for infertility and have thus acquired considerable experience and expertise within the world of achieved conception.

To understand these questions, and to locate the changing discursive construction of 'the facts of life' within the context of lived understandings of these changes, ethnographic interviews were conducted with 20 women undergoing IVF. This fieldwork took place in the West Midlands during 1988 and 1989, and provides a means of relating changes at the level of public, or mainstream culture, to the lives of individuals with direct experience of the world of achieved conception. In the next section data from these interviews are drawn upon in the attempt to illustrate some of the consequences of inhabiting this world, this subculture, and to suggest some of their implications (see further Franklin, 1992).

Making sense of IVF

To begin with, inhabiting the world of achieved conception, defined as it is by certain restricted parameters, opens up a number of gaps which need somehow to be resolved. The most obvious gap is that between the desire for a biological child and the inability to produce one. Related to this is the gap between the biological facts of infertility, which are a definitive component, indeed the foundation of the world of achieved conception, and the social facts of infertility, which are more or less excluded from, or at least marginal to, this world. More specifically, there are gaps in knowledge which often remain unresolved, and a gap between accumulated information and meaningful knowledge which do not always coincide.

Let us consider the last of these examples first. For both the infertile woman and the clinician, particularly in the case of unexplained infertility, *information* which is defined as meaningful, within the parameters of the dominant discourse, does not always add up to meaningful *knowledge*. In interviews with women undergoing IVF, this problem was frequently encountered. A case which illustrates the kind of paradox this can create is that of women who are repeatedly told that 'there is nothing wrong':

> Each test we had they said 'well, everything was fine in there Mrs H., everything was fine', and I kept saying I know you're smiling about this, but I wish you would turn around and say you have found something wrong, because I think in my mind I'd feel easier.

The problem for women such as Mrs H. is that the accumulation of information does not add up to knowledge. The medical information that 'there is nothing wrong' directly contradicts both her knowledge and experience that there is definitely something wrong. Women in the position of Mrs H. invariably know far more technical data about the state of their reproductive physiology than many medical experts, but it serves them little in the way of coming to terms with their condition or doing anything about it.

Another gap which opens up is that between the biological facts of infertility and the social experience of it. Needless to say, infertility is not experienced as a purely biological event. An effect of this is the need somehow to bridge the gap between the technical information given about a woman's physical condition and her experience of infertility as a social condition. It is thus hardly surprising to discover that this need to bridge the gap has the effect of increasing the desire for 'something to be wrong'. The work of coping with the social dimensions of infertility, such as providing explanations to friends, relatives or colleagues for an inability to produce children, or even simply an unwanted absence of them, is eased with the acquisition of some explanation for why conception fails.

The desire for something to be wrong in order for it to be put right is emphasized by the trajectory established by infertility treatment. It is clear in the plumbing analogy and the mechanical sequence which defines the causal chain of biological events leading to conception. Events are *supposed* to proceed along an established path. However, the 'plumbing' turns out to be composed of many mechanisms which are not very clearly understood. This is especially evident in the context of IVF.

Like the standard conception narrative, the procedures involved in assisted conception are initially quite straightforward. Descriptions of IVF need not be overly complex: the egg is removed from the woman's body, fertilized *in vitro* and returned to the womb. In this sense, IVF is represented as a means of replicating, through technological procedures, what 'nature' does 'herself'. However, as the very high failure rates of IVF indicate, the process is far from straightforward. Indeed, many women do not even reach the stage for which IVF is named, fertilization *in vitro*, as there are so many things which can go wrong even before this point in treatment.

As conception is increasingly subject to the clinical and scientific gaze, each stage in the sequence leading to fertilization is broken down into smaller and smaller stages. For 'sperm fertilizes egg' must now be substituted a long list of molecular events which are themselves being subdivided still further as the complex biogenetic process is scrutinized.

The effect of this on conception narratives is to make

them appear more like an obstacle course than a process so simple it could happen if you 'passed him on the stairs'. Far from being as 'easy as falling off a ladder', or as neat 'as shelling peas', conception turns out to be a minor miracle of reproductive physiology. Human reproduction, experts now suggest, 'is remarkably inefficient' (see, for example, Hull, 1986).

IVF is also described as an obstacle course by many of the women who undergo it. For every stage of conception that is broken down into further stages, there are more hurdles to overcome and more things that can eventually go wrong. Conception comes to look more and more like a badly designed process. Not only does nature need a helping hand, it sometimes appears nature would not even get off the starting blocks without the aid of modern technology.

A major component of the experience of IVF is therefore the accumulation of an increasing amount of information about the technical complexity of conception. At one level, this can be very discouraging: as one woman described it to me, IVF is like 'trying to run the Grand National blindfolded and with your legs tied together'. At another level, this has the effect of changing definitions of success and failure in the context of IVF. Initially, success is defined as a successful pregnancy, or a 'take home baby', as it is dubbed. The further a woman goes on with unsuccessful IVF treatment, however, the lower the threshold of relative success drops. Hence, after failing at the first hurdle on the first try, some women may consider their treatment 'successful' if it then moves on to fail at the third hurdle on the second try, or the fourth hurdle on the third try, and so forth. Failure can even be defined as 'successful' treatment if the source of the failure reveals more about the precise problem to be overcome. Hence, for example, a failed treatment which yields diagnostic clarity may be an incentive for a woman to pursue further treatment, as the 'light at the end of the tunnel' becomes more visible, and hope for a successful resolution grows.

IVF is the conception story of the world of achieved conception *par excellence*. Women who undergo this form of treatment are, as Rayna Rapp has noted, reproductive pioneers (Rapp, 1987). It is their bodies in which this domain is being explored by science. It is their lives in which the unprecedented dilemmas posed by treatment, the difficult personal and ethical decisions and choices, are being forged. It is for this reason that the world they inhabit, a world in which the social construction of natural facts takes on a daily, intimate and taxing reality, deserves considered attention. It is also for this reason that the specific dilemmas they face take on a significance that extends well beyond their own immediate circumstances.

This is so not only because public awareness of the number of couples experiencing fertility problems is increasing, but because the world of achieved conception is becoming less and less a subculture and more and more a part of mainstream cultural understandings of parenting, personhood and procreation. Television documentaries, such as 'The World of the Unborn' (*Panorama*, 1988), illustrate the process whereby the meanings produced in the world of achieved conception are becoming more mainstream. In this hour-long documentary, produced by an infertility clinic but aimed at a general audience, conception is no longer the simple biological sequence it used to be. Instead, consistent with the perception of it by infertile couples, conception is represented as an epic saga. The obstacle course analogy prevails. Given the number of things that can go wrong, this documentary would seem to be suggesting, every baby is a miracle baby and it is quite remarkable we can reproduce at all!

A similar example can be drawn from current popular cinema, where an increasing number of films address themselves to the mysteries of procreation. The genres of science fiction and horror in particular have moved from a fascination with outer space to a fascination with inner space. Commenting on such films as *Alien* and *The Fly*, film critic Barbara Creed notes that:

> The sci-fi horror film's current interest in the maternal body and processes of birth points to changes taking place on several fronts. Among the most important of these are the developments taking place in reproductive technology which have put into crisis questions of the subject, the body and the unconscious . . . In more recent years, as experiments with reproductive technology have begun to make enormous headway, [these films] have become increasingly preoccupied with alternative forms of the conception–gestation–birth process. (Creed, 1987: 56–7)

The preoccupation of such films with something going wrong in the conception–gestation–birth process is a clear indication of the widespread anxiety surrounding the current renegotiation of 'the facts of life'. To borrow from the parlance of postmodernism, conception might be thought of as a foundational narrative in crisis. Lost is the certainty and predictability surrounding our maternal origins. Such a loss has understandably disturbing implications.

The changing landscape of reproduction

To appreciate the impact of achieved conception as an emergent cultural construction, it must be situated in the context of broader shifts occurring in the definition of human reproduction. These include the centrality of reproductive processes in general, and of conception in particular, to the rise of biogenetic sciences in recent decades. Also of significance is the increasing medicalization and technologization of the birth process. From this perspective, the 'naturalness' of both human and animal reproduction must be seen as an increasingly residual concept (see Strathern, Chapter 7 below and 1992). As human reproduction becomes increasingly subject to technological monitoring and intervention, now extending from the pre-conception to postnatal stages of the birth process, and plant and animal reproduction become increasingly subject to industrial demands, their 'naturalness' is diminished in relation to their pervasive, patent (and increasingly patented) artificiality.

A second consequence is related to this. The significance of the concept of human achievement in a context previously understood to occur 'naturally' should not be underestimated. As it comes to be seen as less 'natural', so too will conception come to be a less taken-for-granted event. This is already evident in a number of examples. The marketing of ovulation prediction tests, and the rising awareness of the higher-than-expected rates of infertility, coupled with concern about the effects of environmental toxins on fertility, will undoubtedly lead to a more widespread view of conception as an event involving calculated risk and careful reproductive planning. Already this is known as 'pre-conceptive' or 'pre-parental' planning. As more information from the rapidly expanding sciences of biogenetics, concerning the mechanisms of genetic determinism, enters into mainstream cultural circulation, so the events involved in conception will come to be regarded as increasingly significant. Most importantly, they will also be seen as open to increasing degrees of risk, and therefore intervention, such as that already available in the form of pre-implantation diagnosis, a technique designed to select and potentially 'treat' human embryos *in vitro*.

The changing landscape of conception, then, is part of a wider set of changes in the cultural construction of human reproduction. The project to map the human genome now in progress is only one of several components in this refigured field. It is difficult to underestimate the cultural consequences of such changes.

In addition to becoming more complex, more difficult and more subject to technological intervention, conception is also becoming more public. This is true at a number of levels. Conception is now more public in a commercial sense, in so far as reproductive services (as well as reproductive tissue) have become consumer items. It is also more public in that it is now more visible than ever before, and is available in the form of icons, such as that of the unborn fetus or the 'moment' of fertilization, which imagery has now become widely circulated. It is more public also as a form of property, especially in the context of animal husbandry, where the patenting of reproductive techniques and of particular genetic strains or breeds (such as the famous patented mouse) has necessitated the development of gene libraries to accompany already existing gene banks. Finally, conception is moving into the public domain via the mechanisms of state bureaucracy, as evident in regulatory bodies such as the recently created Human Fertilization and Embryology Authority, established in 1990, which oversees licensing arrangements to register clinicians and scientists involved in various forms of assisted conception.

The meaning of assistance

What then of the women who enter the world of assisted conception and are at the cutting edge of a set of techniques which have already precipitated a cultural redefinition of conception to such a great extent? For most women, their venture into this territory will not lead to the desired outcome of a child. The gaps between the social and biological facts of infertility, between information and knowledge, between the desire for a child and the inability to produce one, between the conception narrative they started with and the one they came to inhabit may or may not be resolved. One way or another, they will have to find their way out, as they found their way in, with little support, guidance or precedent to see them through.

It is not therefore surprising to discover that many women have second thoughts about having attempted IVF. Having failed after several attempts, they wonder if they might not have been better able to come to terms with their infertility without it. As one woman said to me, 'Years and years ago, if couples couldn't have children, they just couldn't have children . . . I often wonder if we hadn't started going to fertility clinics right from the beginning, would we not have been better off?' Yet there is an equally strong desire to feel that every possible option has been pursued in the attempt to have a child. Almost always this is phrased in terms of not wanting to look back at a later stage in life and feel there was something that could have been tried and might have succeeded. On the one hand, new forms of technological assistance offer the possibility, however remote, of success-ful pregnancy. On the other hand, the costs of these largely unsuccessful forms of reproductive assistance are virtually impossible to gauge at the outset. Such are the dilemmas an increasing number of would-be parents will face, be it in the context of infertility treatment, prenatal diagnosis or in the proposed treatment of genetic disorders, all of which involve a reproductive experience which is mediated by technology.

If conception stories are cultural cosmologies in micro-cosm, then the conception story of IVF, of the world of achieved conception, deserves comment not only because it is limited in terms of therapeutic success. The limits it imposes are also limits of cultural imagination. As the dominant analogies from the world of achieved conception become more definitive of human reproduction in general – the analogies of scientific achievement, of technological assistance, of mechanical sequences, or of an obstacle course – so too do our definitions of kinship and personhood alter accordingly. For example, as Marilyn Strathern has noted (see Chapter 7), it is unclear how the meaning of assistance in the domain of kinship will alter understandings of fundamental social ties. Such shifts are already evident in statutory definitions of 'mothers', 'fathers' and 'pregnan-cies', which, by the very process of attempting to define these terms, paradoxically bring to the fore their increasing ambiguity. Similar shifts are also evident in redefinitions of the natural facts of pregnancy and childbirth, such as the redefinition of the 'embryo' as the 'pre-embryo'. Most of all, they are evident in the dilemmas faced by infertile couples undergoing IVF, but already these are dilemmas which are facing a much wider population.

Conclusion

Looking back to the curiosity expressed by Victorian anthropologists at the puzzling conception stories of the Trobrianders, there can be seen, perhaps, a different object lesson. Instead of a culture so divergent from our own, there is a familiar pattern. In the negotiation of conception stories our most powerful cultural idioms can be seen at work: of industrialism, technology, scientific progress, the advance of knowledge and the ability to control and improve natural processes for the betterment of humankind. Moreover, we see conception located in a matrix of social institutions which give it the specific meanings through which it makes sense to us, including those of medicine, law, commerce and the state. Were a visitor from Kiriwina to visit us today, in a reverse pilgrimage to that of Malinowski, he or she would likely arrive at the same conclusion: that conception stories do indeed reveal a culture's definition of itself. And such a visitor would have to be forgiven too for commenting on Malinowski's view of the Trobrianders as quite exotic in their accounts of human conception. Had Malinowski been a member of the Warnock Committee, his fieldnotes would have been copious indeed.

References

Bellina, J. and Wilson, J. (1986) *The Fertility Handbook: a Positive and Practical Guide*. Harmondsworth: Penguin.

Creed, B. (1987) 'From Here to Modernity: feminism and postmodernism', *Screen*, 28(2): 47–67.

Delaney, C. (1986) 'The meaning of paternity and the virgin birth debate', *Man*, 21: 494–513.

Foucault, M. (1977) *The History of Sexuality*. Harmondsworth: Penguin.

Franklin, S. (1992) *Contested Conceptions: a Cultural Account of Assisted Reproduction*. PhD thesis. Department of Cultural Studies, University of Birmingham.

Hull, M.G.R. (1986) 'Infertility: nature and extent of problem', in CIBA Foundation, *Human Embryo Research: Yes or No*. London: Tavistock, pp. 24–35.

Laqueur, T. (1986) 'Orgasm, generation and the politics of reproductive biology', *Representations*, 14: 1–41.

Leach, E. (1966) 'Virgin birth', *Proceedings of the Royal Anthropological Institute for 1966*, pp. 39–49.

Malinowski, B. (1916) 'Baloma: the spirits of the dead in the Trobriand Islands', *Journal of the Royal Anthropological Institute*, 46: 353–430.

Malinowski, B. (1925) *The Father in Primitive Society*. New York: Harcourt, Brace and World.

Malinowski, B. (1929) *The Sexual Life of Savages in North-Western Melanesia*. London: Routledge and Kegan Paul.

Martin, E. (1991) 'The Egg and the Sperm', *Signs*, 16(3): 485–501.

Montagu, A. (1937) *Coming into Being Among the Australian Aborigines*. London: Routledge and Kegan Paul.

Panorama (1988) 'The World of the Unborn', Genesis Productions. Transmitted BBC1.

Rapp, R. (1987) 'Moral pioneers: women, men and fetuses on a frontier of reproductive technology', *Women and Health*, 13(1/2): 101–16.

Spiro, M. (1968) 'Virgin birth, pathenogenesis and physiological paternity: an essay in cultural interpretation', *Man*, 3: 242–61.

Strathern, M. (1992) *After Nature: English Kinship in the Late Twentieth Century*. Cambridge: Cambridge University Press.

Weiner, A. (1976) *Women of Value, Men of Renown: New Perspectives in Trobriand Exchange*. Austin, TX: University of Texas Press.

Weiner, A. (1988) *The Trobrianders of Papua New Guinea*. Orlando, FL: Holt, Rinehart and Winston.

5

Having triplets, quads or quins: who bears the responsibility?

FRANCES PRICE

> I can really understand it [all becoming too much], you know. I really can. Because if you haven't got any help and you haven't got any money and you've no space – I think these three things, I could, I mean even now, with all the help we've got, there are days when I could walk out.
>
> (Mother of triplets: interview transcript, National Triplet Study)

It is difficult to envisage contemporary children being protected as wards of royalty as were the Dionne quintuplets born in an isolated farmhouse in Ontario, Canada in 1934 (Berton, 1977). Within the space of a few years *Time* magazine reported them as the world's greatest news picture story.[1] Inspiring excitement and curiosity around the world, these five identical children, Emille, Yvonne, Cecile, Marie and Annette, were made wards of King George VI. A seven-bedroom house was built for them by the Canadian government. However, this did not protect them from becoming a commercial peepshow. Even before they reached the age of five, they had been viewed from behind a one-way screen by some two million people.

To conceive, deliver, nurture and care for triplets,

quadruplets, quintuplets or more – children of higher order multiple births – is an extraordinary situation for any woman to confront. With only two breasts, arms, hands, knees and feet, a woman is not fashioned to breastfeed or knee-bounce triplets, quadruplets, quintuplets or more. There are those who find this mismatch deeply disturbing. As the Human Fertilization and Embryology Bill moved through Parliament in 1990, one member of the House of Commons referred to 'the awful problem of the birth of litters'.

When Patti Frustaci gave birth to septuplets in California in 1985, the image of her husband Sam hugging her obstetrician was transmitted around the world. 'It's a neat experience. Family life is great,' Sam Frustaci reportedly exclaimed. His ebullience was to be short lived.

Few women and men can envisage the situation: the magnitude of the responsibilities and the ways in which the familiar is rendered unfamiliar. In the United Kingdom, once a mother and her three or more babies are discharged from hospital, there is no structured provision for the cumulative consequences. And there is all too often a disordering of relationships in this extraordinary childcare situation.

This chapter is about the demonstrable uncertainties not only surrounding the bearing, rearing and provision for triplets, quads and more but also in locating responsibility for this outcome when it arises following medical assistance in the quest for a pregnancy. In the context of the new reproductive technologies, these uncertainties are of wider contemporary concern. They raise fundamental questions about the authority of the decision making involved in this area of medicine where clinicians, the majority of whom work in the private sector, are encouraged to provide whatever services are deemed to be within the ambit of medical competence. To make the case that these decisions are not solely medical matters (cf. Kennedy, 1988) is just the starting point for the sociologist.

Incidence of triplets or more

Three, four, five, six, seven and more babies may be born of the same pregnancy. A case of nonoplets (nine) is probably the largest recorded multiple birth: none of the infants survived. But pregnancies with more than three fetuses are rare. Working with German statistics at the turn of the century, Hellin suggested a formula by which the incidence of higher multiple births in a given population could be calculated: if n is the incidence of twins in a population, n^2 is that of triplets, n^3 is that of quadruplets and so on (Hellin, 1895). On this basis, populations such as those in Europe and North America where one set of twins is born once in about 100 deliveries, the incidence of triplets should be one in 10,000 and that of quadruplets one in one million. Other studies in the first half of this century appeared to support this mathematical relationship.

Missing from Hellin's formulations, however, was any distinction between the incidence of different types of twins, triplets and quadruplets and more. These children may arise from two, three or more separate zygotes (each the product of the fertilization of one sperm with one egg) or from a single zygote which divides, or from a combination of the two.

Very little is known about the reasons for separation within a single zygote. Yet separation into two (a monozygotic or identical pair) is remarkably constant across all human populations: about 3.5 deliveries per thousand. The constancy of the incidence of monozygosity contrasts with the marked variations around the world in twins, triplets and more which arise from the fertilization of separate eggs (dizygotic, trizygotic or higher order zygosity or non-identical twins, triplets or higher order birth children). Rates of non-identical twinning are particularly high in parts of Africa, such as Nigeria, and particularly low in Japan. There may be a genetic predisposition to multiple ovulation, which perhaps is modified by environmental factors. Also, the likelihood of a woman releasing several eggs which fertilize and develop with a multiple birth as an outcome increases both with advancing age, peaking in her late 30s, and with parity, that is the larger the number of children she has previously borne.

What is of far greater significance in considering the incidence of multiple births, however, is the unpredictable impact of developments in the medical management of infertility since the mid 1960s – in particular the rapid rise in the number of triplets and higher order births around the world. In England and Wales, 183 sets of triplets, 11 sets of quadruplets and one set of quintuplets were born in 1989, compared with 70 sets of triplets and 6 sets of quadruplets in 1982: 28.6 sets per 100,000 deliveries in 1989 compared with 12.2 per 100,000 in 1982.

'Fertility' drugs

The principal objective in the medical management of infertility is to enable a woman to conceive. As some infertility problems arise as a consequence of a failure to ovulate, a common first-line strategy to achieve this objective has been to attempt to induce ovulation, although it does not by any means follow that conception will, or can, occur subsequently. Ovulation is the result of a finely coordinated interaction between hypothalamic, pituitary and ovarian hormones and the causes of anovulatory states can be far from straightforward – quite apart from the complexity of various other menstrual cycle disturbances.

There is now ample evidence, however, that certain ovarian stimulants are associated with an incidence of multiple gestation well above the spontaneous occurrence rate. The recent increase in the number of triplets and more is a consequence. The drugs that are in established clinical use are very likely to stimulate multiple ovulation: more than one ovarian follicle develops and ruptures, and a number of eggs are released. If two or more are fertilized a multiple pregnancy is then possible. In studies published between 1953 and 1976, rates of multiple ovulation after induction of ovulation by gonadotrophins were reported as ranging between 18 and 53.5 per cent (Schenker et al., 1981).

One ovarian stimulant that has been in use for well over a quarter of a century is the drug clomiphene citrate (Clomid, Serophene). A relatively inexpensive ovulatory induction agent which can be prescribed by general practitioners, this drug has been shown to be effective in a wide range of anovulatory states such as hypothalamic–pituitary dysfunction, polycystic ovary disorder, post-oral contraceptive amenorrhoea and postpartum amenorrhoea. All the early reports of this drug noted a good response in terms of ovarian follicle numbers after stimulation but a relatively small risk of a multiple gestation (Murray and Osmond-Clark, 1971). The manufacturer of Clomid states that the drug is associated with a 6–8 per cent risk of a multiple pregnancy.

The risk of a multiple pregnancy is greater, however, with another drug in frequent use in specialist practice: human menopausal gonadotrophin (Pergonal). This drug is given by intramuscular injections in conjunction with human chorionic gonadotrophin (Profasi). The prescribing information for Pergonal provided by the manufacturer asserts that 'the incidence of multiple births following Pergonal/Profasi therapy has been variously reported between 10 per cent and 40 per cent: the majority of multiple conceptions are twins' (Serono Laboratories, 1986).

Refinements in gonadotrophin administration – utilizing improved hormone monitoring by rapid assays and high resolution ovarian ultrasound scanning to monitor the growth of the follicles – may have lowered the risk of a multiple pregnancy somewhat. But treatments are difficult to monitor. The difficulty of controlling the number of follicles that develop in response to this and other ovulation-inducing drugs and the consequent risk of such a pregnancy remains.

In recent years, some clinics report that they have improved their pregnancy rate per treatment cycle by combining ovulation stimulation with intrauterine insemination (IUI). The rationale for this approach is to bypass the cervical barrier by depositing large numbers of washed, mobile sperm directly into the woman's uterus. Overstimulation of the ovaries is an acknowledged drawback. Figures published in June 1991 by the Hallam Medical Centre indicate that between 6 and 7 per cent of women undergoing IUI produce more than four follicles. The clinic's multiple pregnancy rate for treatment cycles with ovarian stimulation with IUI was higher than for treatment cycles with ovarian stimulation alone: 'out of the first 100 pregnancies resulting from our IUI programme, nine were multiple pregnancies, seven twins and two triplets'.[2]

Several well-publicized 'grand multiple' births and deaths have promoted public awareness that the acceptance of certain forms of medical assistance in the quest for a pregnancy may have untoward consequences. Widespread publicity was given to the aforementioned Frustacis and their septuplets in 1985. Following the birth of their first child, conceived after Patti Frustaci had taken a fertility drug, the couple sought medical assistance for the second time. Her septuplet pregnancy followed a course of Pergonal. One septuplet was stillborn, three died within 19 days, and the three survivors all have impaired vision and are developmentally delayed. Soon after the birth of their seven babies, the parents instigated malpractice litigation on the grounds that the Pergonal dosage was too high and the obstetric monitoring by ultrasonography inadequate.[3]

Two years later, in 1987, Susan Halton gave birth to septuplets in Liverpool. No child lived longer than 16 days. A simple headstone in a cemetery in Merseyside records the date of death of each child. The birth and early death, despite intensive neonatal care, of all the Halton septuplets created intense public and professional consternation. Both tragedies served to heighten the professional concern that induction of ovulation is not always monitored adequately.

Multiple egg and embryo transfer

A more recent concern is the rate of multiple pregnancies after doctors have transferred several eggs or embryos in assisted conception techniques such as *in vitro* fertilization (IVF) and gamete intrafallopian transfer (GIFT). Many clinics practising IVF and GIFT have achieved both high rates of egg recovery and of fertilization. But, although early development of such embryos is satisfactory, the rates of implantation remain low. The vigour of research and the considerable publicity surrounding births following IVF and GIFT belies the low success rate in establishing clinical pregnancies (ILA, 1991).

There is considerable dissent about what constitutes 'good practice' in the field of IVF and GIFT. This turns, in part, on different evaluations of acknowledged clinical risks, on what is to count as evidence, on the professional priority to be given in each clinical case to establishing and maintaining a pregnancy and on whether it is possible to predict which women are at greater risk of a multiple birth. Certain IVF clinics encourage the idea of a multiple birth by including photographs of twins and triplets in their publicity material.

In the early 1980s, it was asserted that the IVF pregnancy rate would increase with the number of embryos transferred in each treatment cycle (Biggers, 1981). Edwards later put forward the idea, since retracted, that a synergism exists which he called embryo 'helping': an embryo capable of implantation somehow facilitates other transferred embryos to implant (Edwards, 1985). By the mid 1980s, pooled counts from IVF centres around the world seemed to confirm such predictions and encouraged the transfer of between three and six embryos (Seppala, 1985). If at least three embryos are transferred, Steptoe estimated the risk of a multiple pregnancy at about 25 per cent and raised the question 'Are the risks of high multiparity justified?' (Steptoe, 1986). However, it appears that the marked increase in triplet and higher order multiple pregnancies from 1985 onwards was not envisaged.

From 1986 onwards, shortages of both staff and cots in hospital intensive care units made the difficulties of neonatal provision for these children even more apparent. Neonatal paediatricians voiced their concern at conferences, in letters to professional journals and in letters to Ministers of State about the increased incidence of triplet and higher order multiple births and their effects on neonatal services (Anderson, 1987; Levene, 1986, 1991; Peters et al., 1991; Scott-Jupp et al., 1991).

Better access to ovarian follicles with ultrasound-guided retrieval along with new combinations of ovulatory drugs, have enabled larger numbers of eggs to be collected. In 1988, six or more eggs were collected in almost half of all IVF treatment cycles in which a pregnancy was established in Australia and New Zealand (National Perinatal Statistics Unit, 1990). Some 80 per cent of the resulting pregnancies occurred after the transfer of three or more embryos. A triplet pregnancy remains a possible, if unlikely, outcome.

The dilemma lies here: because the transfer of three embryos or eggs in IVF and GIFT is believed to offer the best chance of a pregnancy, it is now regarded internationally as the 'normal' practice. In the United Kingdom, one-third of all triplet births in 1989 followed after IVF and 10 per cent after GIFT (ILA, 1991).

The annual statistics produced in the United Kingdom by the Interim Licensing Authority for Human *In Vitro* Fertilization and Embryology (ILA, formerly the Voluntary Licensing Authority, VLA) show a clear association between the rise of multiple births from 1985 onward and the increased use of IVF, GIFT and associated procedures (ILA, 1991). The Medical Research Council (MRC) Working Party on Children Conceived by *In Vitro* Fertilization found that 23 per cent of deliveries following assisted conception by IVF and GIFT resulted in a multiple birth of twins or more, compared with about 1 per cent for natural conceptions (MRC, 1990). There is an additional risk factor: a higher than expected frequency of identical (monozygotic) twins, not only after the induction of ovulation with drugs, but also after IVF and GIFT (Derom et al., 1987; Edwards et al., 1986). Thus there are reports of three eggs or embryos being transferred in a GIFT or IVF procedure and the outcome being a quadruplet pregnancy.

In 1987 the ILA guidelines stated that no more than three eggs or embryos should be transferred in any one cycle unless there are exceptional clinical reasons when up to four eggs or embryos may be transferred (VLA, 1987). Of the 1,092 deliveries following assisted conception by IVF or GIFT in the MRC Working Party study period, an average of 2.9 embryos were transferred for each IVF delivery and 6.3 ova for each GIFT delivery (MRC, 1990). Most (92 per cent) of the GIFT deliveries occurred in 1987, the year in which the Authority's guideline about the recommended maximum number of eggs and embryos was announced.

The results for 1988 from ILA-licensed clinics indicated that the majority of clinics had restricted the number of embryos transferred to three; however, 'one large clinic transferred four [embryos] in over 60 per cent of cases' (ILA, 1990). By 1989, despite the ILA guideline about exceptional circumstances, 9.9 per cent of all IVF transfers were of four or more embryos (ILA, 1990). And in the case of GIFT:

> 59 per cent of all cases had four or more eggs transferred. This is of particular concern in that the transfer of five or more eggs results in a multiple pregnancy rate of 41.7 per cent without a significant increase in the pregnancy rate. (ILA, 1991: 18)

In August 1991, the newly established Human Fertilization and Embryology Authority (HFEA), set up under the terms of the 1990 Human Fertilization and Embryology Act, published a Code of Practice stating that three embryos were the maximum to be transferred in any one cycle. Monitoring of the GIFT procedure, however, is not covered by the remit of the HFEA, unless the procedure involves the use of donated eggs or sperm. The framing of the 1990 Act only covers research and clinical practice involving work with embryos. If there has been no donation the GIFT procedure is excluded because it involves clinical work with eggs and sperm.

At least two of the larger licensed assisted conception centres in the United Kingdom have data that demonstrate that pregnancy rates are just as high when the number of embryos transferred is limited to two (when more than two are available) as they are when three are transferred (Waterstone et al., 1991). Alternatives to drug-stimulated IVF – in particular the close monitoring of the hormonal fluctuations within a woman's natural menstrual cycle – are available in some centres. This enables the time of ovulation to be predicted so that the retrieval of a single mature egg can be assured with a high degree of confidence. Called 'natural cycle IVF', this procedure is far less stressful and is undertaken entirely on an outpatient basis. But it requires expertise in endocrinology and, as yet, the pregnancy rate is appreciably lower than the rate obtained in IVF programmes using ovarian stimulation.[4]

Expectations

Few data exist on what people attending infertility clinics expect from the clinical services they might receive. However, women and men confronting infertility may view a multiple pregnancy in a positive light. At the Universitaire Baudelocque in Paris, most (90 per cent) couples in the IVF programme were ready to take the risk of a triplet outcome to maximize their chances of a pregnancy (Contrepas, 1989). Some 7 per cent of people attending the clinic expressed reservations about the possibility of multiple pregnancy and a few (3 per cent), declared themselves incapable of envisaging bringing up twins, quite apart from triplets. In an unpublished survey in New Jersey, Leiblum and her co-workers report that of four groups of women (designated 'IVF, ovulation stimulation with human gonadotrophins (hMG), donor insemination and female medical student'), the 'IVF women' were 'the most receptive to having quadruplets or even quintuplets rather than having no biological children' (Leiblum et al., 1989).

Few people have known children from a triplet, quadruplet or higher order set. Even fewer have produced care or support for these children, for their parents and for any siblings. For most people, the prospect of triplets or more is too remote to be imaginable. Ignorance seems understandable: the problems faced by those responsible for their delivery, care and welfare are not widely known. When, however, clinicians advocate procedures that increase the risk of plural births, this ignorance becomes disconcerting.

Triplets, quadruplets and higher order birth children bring unusual stresses and are, in all senses, high cost (Mugford, 1990; Price, 1991). They are more likely than single infants to be of low birth weight and to be born prematurely, with all the associated neonatal difficulties, increased risk of disability and continuing developmental problems (Macfarlane et al., 1990a).

The National Study

Little has been known about the coping strategies of parents of triplets, quadruplets and more, nor about the extent to which they can elicit support and help from friends, relatives and outside agencies. In the late 1980s, as the rise in the numbers of these births became more marked in the United

Kingdom in national registration data, and as paediatricians became more vocal about the neonatal consequences, all these concerns led to support from the Department of Health for a national study. This has now provided the first comprehensive data from Britain. Called the United Kingdom Study of Triplets and Higher Order Births (The National Study), it is also the first study in the world to look at the problems to be faced in caring for these children (Botting et al., 1990).

The study was designed to provide more information and to look for ways of improving the care and services provided for parents with children from triplet and higher order births. Information was collected, in three complementary surveys, of the problems encountered by parents and by the doctors concerned with 313 sets of triplets and 27 sets of quadruplets, quintuplets or sextuplets born in the early to mid 1980s. Surveys of obstetricians, paediatricians, other specialists and of family doctors were conducted jointly by the Office of Population, Censuses and Surveys (OPCS) in London and the National Perinatal Epidemiology Unit (NPEU) in Oxford. I undertook the survey of parents (the Parents' Study) which was based at the Child Care and Development Group of the University of Cambridge (Price, 1991).

The Parents' Study involved the mothers, and many of the fathers, of triplets, quadruplets and quintuplets born in the years 1979–88. Above all, the study was intended to obtain information about the specific needs and problems of these parents, their sources of assistance, advice and benefits in kind. Parents' own views about the type, quality and timing of the help and support were central to the study.

Some women in the Parents' Study emphasized that their triplets or quads were 'natural', a chance event. They wanted to make clear that they were to be distinguished from other women who, it seemed to them, had made a choice in seeking specific clinical services in reproductive medicine which were associated with the risk of a multiple birth. In allocating responsibility for the birth, the distinction between a 'natural' and an 'artificial' cause was made. The many ramifications of such a distinction and the difficulties with attributions of responsibility and with the idea of choice in this matter formed the backcloth to the National Study, as did the debates and divisions among clinicians and scientists engaged in the provision of services for people diagnosed as infertile.

Death and disability

In the National Study over half of the quadruplets and just over a quarter of the triplets weighed less than 1,500 g at birth. About half the quadruplet or higher order births included in the obstetric survey occurred before 32 weeks' gestation compared with a quarter of triplets and less than a tenth of twins. In contrast, only 1 per cent of singletons sampled in the Maternity Hospital In-Patient Enquiry were born before 32 weeks' gestation (Macfarlane et al., 1990b).

More triplets, quadruplets and quintuplets now survive than was the case in the 1970s and earlier, but their mortality rates have not fallen as rapidly as those for single births. Figures for England and Wales suggest that their risk of stillbirth is about six times that for singletons, and the risk of death in the first year is about ten times higher (Botting et al., 1987).

Compared with singletons, triplets and higher order birth children have a higher rate of serious congenital malformations visible at birth (Macfarlane et al., 1990a). Notified malformations of the central nervous system and of the cardiovascular system are about twice as common among multiple birth children as among singletons. Complications of prematurity and uteroplacental insufficiency are the main contributors to perinatal morbidity and mortality. These children are at an increased risk of cerebral palsy, particularly spastic diplegia, squint, pyloric stenosis and repeated hospital admissions.

Demanding childcare

When the children come home from hospital, their care-takers face a very demanding situation: it is not possible for one person to cope alone for any length of time (Price, 1990a). Where space is confined it is likely to become an issue of great consequence and difficulties with transport can be an impediment to outings (Price, 1990b). Mothers of triplets and more risk becoming isolated and housebound, particularly in the first two years, if they have neither someone with whom to share the responsibility for the children nor a companion to accompany them on outings to parks and play areas (Price, 1990a).

Reported difficulties are emotional as well as practical. One mother of two-year-old triplets described the difficulties of coping without respite from her children:

> Now they have reached two years and two months I find that they are becoming a handful, and my patience with them is wearing very thin. This is in spite of the fact that I have access to a car, and get out and about with them every day. I am quite firm with them and will take no nonsense, have an excellent routine which allows me free time in the afternoon whilst they sleep for a couple of hours, and are in bed by 7 o'clock in the evening. The problems seem to arise from the fact that I get no respite from them at all. My husband freely admits that he cannot cope with them either emotionally or physically, and friends feel intimidated with the sheer number of them to cope . . .
>
> I suppose the bickering and whining is quite normal for children of this age – but multiplied by three tends to eat into your brain. As you can well imagine, this bickering

tends to spill over into my husband and I having a go at each other, and our relationship is under a great deal of strain.

Familiar timetables are disrupted, and relationships also. Seldom are these consequences anticipated. The situation is not normal: attempts to behave 'as normal' usually have untoward consequences, especially when the parents' exhaustion is exacerbated by insufficient sleep (Price, 1991). Mothers of triplets in the study described the feelings of being 'a freak':

> I am, I suppose, a private person and I have found the amount of attention they attract difficult to cope with. I can't walk down the main street without people approaching me. At times people do, probably unwittingly, make you feel a bit of a freak.
>
> I would not like the last three and a half years again. I have got very annoyed with people in the street who think we are so different and ask the same old questions. I have found myself becoming very withdrawn and rude to a point where I don't stop when people stop me.

Three, four or more same-age, language-learning infants are clamouring for adult attention. Turn-taking has to be learnt and the situation is extraordinarily stressful. One mother of triplets wrote:

> The thing I found was we were so busy caring for the triplets, we didn't find the time to enjoy them. The aim in the day was to get them to bed at night.

Mothers identified several priorities: assistance with childcare, from whatever source, particularly with night- and day-time feeding in the first year, together with help to get out of the house and to enable children to go to some form of preschool in the second and third year. They wanted reliable, practical help; resources to ensure that they could continue to carry out their responsibilities; support on a day-to-day basis and appropriate professional support. But, in order to ask for practical help and support, they needed to know what sources of help or kind of services would meet their sense of need. Such services and sources of help, in practice, were all too often unavailable.

Such is the novelty of the situation and scale of the demands that the help, support and advice available from the health and social services, and also from the voluntary sector, may not begin to meet the needs as perceived by the parents. One local authority social services department manager summed it up by saying:

> Such cases do not easily 'fit' in terms of local authority provision – i.e. not elderly, not handicapped, no real question of reception into care. Require some 'imaginative' and liberal interpretation of guidelines and legislation.

Also these services are already stretched both as a consequence of welfare policies transferring care to the community and a shortage of volunteers.

At the heart of the matter is the question of who can provide what time to help, when and at what cost. It could not be taken for granted that relatives would rally round. Relatives were not always able, or willing, to help, although most of the mothers in the Parents' Study had at least one relative on whom they relied for support and practical help in the crucial early months after some or all of their triplets or quadruplets came home from hospital. But few relatives could provide sustained help and support beyond this time.

More than half of the parents reported that their relatives had difficulty providing assistance because of their age, infirmity, distance or lack of transport. Not many parents could rely on relatives for long-term help and support on a daily basis. In addition, fewer than half of the parents recorded that they had one or more friend or neighbour who had provided regular support and practical help during the first year. About a third of the parents had no help from relatives, friends or neighbours in the first year after the birth. A mother of IVF triplets in the Parents' Study described the difficulties of being bereft of helpers:

> At times it has been very difficult to get out and about, especially now that the trio are two and a half and are wanting to walk. It is very difficult to control (for their own safety) three tiny children when out. Helpers in our case are very few and far between, as most friends have since returned to work after having had their families and family help is too far away. At times it can seem like an *existence* or *sentence*. (Emphasis in original)

The problems did not end when the children went to school. Although most of the children from triplet and higher order births in the study had some experience of playgroup or nursery school, many had little experience of separation from each other. Some of them were markedly dependent on each other, and at the time of their entry to school this posed a problem for their teachers, who were unlikely to have experience in dealing with triplets or more.

Mothers and fathers of multiple birth children are unlikely to be any less active than are parents of singletons in promoting the welfare and optimum development of all their children. But their circumstances are significantly different from the parents of singletons. The situation is not just comparable to one in which there is one adult and one child, or one adult and different-aged children. Attempting to develop coping strategies to provide each child with individual attention was stressful, particularly when one or more child had special needs, or required sustained extra help with, for instance, speech therapy exercises, reading or numeracy (Price et al., 1990).

Tailoring multiparity

For some years now, when a woman has been diagnosed to

have a triplet or higher order multiple pregnancy, there has been an alternative to complete termination. If she cannot face the prospect of bringing up three or more children then a partial termination is possible in the first trimester. This procedure is known as 'selective feticide', 'selective birth' or, more recently, 'selective reduction'. The usual procedure involves a lethal injection of potassium chloride into the heart of one or more of the fetuses until cardiac activity ceases. The operation involves passing a needle through the pregnant woman's abdomen. An ultrasound image of the fetuses in the womb enables the clinician to view what is happening. The procedure is technically difficult, however, as it requires the precise placement of a needle in a very small area. If the pregnancy continues the dead fetuses become compressed by the fetuses that continue to develop and are delivered with the placenta.

Although the practice is not widespread, it has been employed in the United States and the United Kingdom for more than a decade in situations following prenatal diagnosis of severe abnormality or genetic anomaly (Aberg et al., 1978; Rodeck et al., 1982). In such cases the development of the abnormal twin is brought to a halt, usually some time after the fourth month of pregnancy, with the hope that the surviving twin will flourish. But there has been legal uncertainty: the decision not to prosecute an obstetrician who undertook the procedure in a case involving a 27-week twin fetus with Klinefelter's syndrome[5] in 1989 was not settled until 1991 (Dyer, 1991).

The use of selective reduction on grounds of *number*, rather than on grounds of abnormality, is more recent. The first published report of selective reduction in a higher order multiple pregnancy was in 1986; a quintuplet gestation in the Netherlands was reduced to twins which resulted in the birth of two healthy females at term (Kanhai et al., 1986). Other selective reductions have been reported subsequently in the United Kingdom, France, Australia, Germany and the United States.

In a case reported from Australia, eight gestational sacs and seven fetal hearts were detected in a woman who had four eggs transferred in the GIFT procedure (Yovitch et al., 1988). The possibilities that could lead to this occurrence include the division of the four eggs after fertilization (multiple monozygosity) or delayed spontaneous ovulation after the GIFT procedure was completed. Four fetuses were sacrificed by a cardiotoxic injection at nine weeks' gestation. But the 'triplet' pregnancy miscarried in the eighteenth week.

There is no public record in the United Kingdom of the number of selective reductions undertaken. Obstetricians are wary of the procedure and it is difficult in some countries to find an obstetrician to undertake it. To some extent legal uncertainties were assuaged in the United Kingdom when the Human Fertilization and Embryology Act of 1990 brought selective reduction under the Abortion Act.

At least one clinician in the United Kingdom is prepared to offer this procedure to women who are not already under his care, and others have stated that they would be prepared to consider the procedure for women already under their supervision (Bryan, 1990). In France, by contrast, several clinics make selective reduction routinely available to women with triplet or higher order pregnancies (Bryan, 1990).

The obstetric advantages of fetal reduction have been discussed in the medical literature, as have the ethical issues (Wapner et al., 1990). But there has been no systematic study of the experience of those who have undergone the procedure. Articles in the press and in support group newsletters indicate the concerns and confusions (Anonymous, 1989; Bryan, 1989; Steven, 1989; Varley, 1989).

Bryan's study conducted in the mid 1980s focused on the experiences of 11 of the first 13 women to undergo this procedure for twin pregnancies where one twin but not the other had some abnormality likely to cause severe physical or mental disability (twin–twin discordancy) (Bryan, 1989).

All had undergone the procedure at 18–31 weeks of pregnancy at one centre in England. All now had one surviving child. None had known about selective reduction before the diagnosis.

Bryan suggested that the medical profession was in general insufficiently informed about selective reduction; that it failed to give appropriate advice; and that the sense of loss at the time of the birth was neither acknowledged nor supported. Only one woman was offered bereavement counselling. Some women had to explain the procedures to their general practitioner, health visitor and midwife. Of the 11 women, nine had told close relatives and friends, some of whom were disturbed by the idea. One woman who had undergone the procedure was distressed by the horrified reaction of her friends. Only one was not planning to tell her surviving child. The rest were concerned about how best to explain what had occurred.

This is a problematic option for a pregnant woman. She may accept the procedure with relief but later experience grief and guilt. Her partner may accept the option more readily and bring pressure to bear. No one has yet explored the psychological and social complications for the parents and the survivors. There is an inherent ambivalence. One life or more may be 'destroyed', 'spared' or transformed. Any distress is compounded by the fact that few people are aware of the technique, or of the reasons for which it might be offered (*Lancet*, 1988).

Issues of even greater complexity are presented by a case in Italy where GIFT, genetic diagnosis and selective reduction were undertaken to enable twins to be born in 1990 to a woman and her partner who risked passing on β-thalassaemia to their offspring (Brambati et al., 1990). All eight eggs recovered from the woman in the GIFT procedure were transferred with the intention of increasing 'the likelihood of a multiple pregnancy'. At six weeks a quadruplet pregnancy was diagnosed and, after genetic diagnosis, the four embryos were reduced to two. The medical team report that the woman subsequently 'was delivered by caesarian section of a healthy 2,300 g boy and a 2,430 g girl' at 37 weeks' gestation (Brambati et al., 1990).

How many is too many?

The precise extent to which the marked rise in higher order multiple pregnancies can be attributed to the drugs and procedures in the management of infertility is not known. There is no dispute, however, that triplet and greater order pregnancies have increased in incidence in line with the provision of assisted conception. Annual documentation for Australia and New Zealand and also for the United Kingdom demonstrates the magnitude of the increase.

There are those clinicians who regard these pregnancies as a disaster for all concerned, besides spelling trouble for paediatric units. These doctors urge strongly that all possible steps should be taken to ensure that the risk of such a pregnancy is avoided. Views differ, however, about good practice in this burgeoning field of medicine and questions about how many embryos and eggs to transfer in assisted conception procedures and about selective reduction on grounds of number remain at the forefront of controversy. Some clinicians regard both these contested zones as matters solely for clinical judgement.

Change is anticipated: there is regulation and review. Yet in the policy arena, certainly in the United Kingdom, ideas about the standing of medical decisions in clinical practice remain highly influential and pave the way for certain policy conclusions. Institutional pressures protect the privileged status of clinical judgement which is used to control the discourse about risk. Medical practitioners are accustomed both to being authoritative in decision-making and to having autonomous control of their activities.

There is a concern that people seeking such clinical services are enabled to make more informed reproductive decisions and to assume responsibility for envisaging the possible consequences for their lives. But here lies the dilemma. The transfer of three embryos or eggs is generally regarded, internationally, as 'normal' practice in IVF and GIFT for the best chance of a pregnancy. This also seems to be the practice for a fertile woman undergoing IVF surrogacy. At least two women have undergone IVF and have borne triplets for another woman (Reid, 1988).

Will selective reduction of multiple pregnancy become more generally available and if so under what circumstances and for what order of multiplicity? Are twins to be regarded as a normal pregnancy outcome, or not? The public policy issues in this field go beyond declarations that there should be an increased consumer voice and consumer choice in medicine. The extent to which the communication of information about these matters is in disarray has been effectively masked. Long-standing notions not only about the hermetic nature of the doctor–patient relationship but also about clinical freedom have powerfully structured the agenda for debate, particularly in relation to establishing guidelines, to external regulation, to informed consent and to the nature and extent of counselling at the 'interface' between doctor and patient.

Within the clinics, different social relations get translated into questions of biology, the promotional language is of remedy and the problem for sociologists is to forge new conceptual frameworks. Far more than facilitation of pregnancy is at issue. The significance of these acts of assistance extends beyond the prospect of pregnancy, birth and the associated clinical risks and uncertainties. Women and men now shoulder new kinds of risk and uncertainty concerning their future relationships, particularly if there has been a multiple birth or a selective reduction.

Notes

I am very grateful to Jill Brown, Naomi Pfeffer and Meg Stacey for their help with this chapter. The Parents' Study of the National Study of Triplets and Higher Order Births was supported by the Department of Health under its Small Grants Scheme (JS 240/85/13) and could not have been completed without the help and support of Beverley Botting and Alison Macfarlane.

1 *Time*, 11 January 1937.
2 The Hallam Medical Centre's information sheet 'Intra-uterine Insemination with Superovulation', 18 June 1991.
3 The law suit was settled out of court in July 1990 with the fertility clinic agreeing to pay the Frustacis $450,000 and give the three surviving children monthly payments.
4 The pregnancy rate depends on the cause of the infertility. Patricia Kohn of the Sheffield Fertility Centre reports that in 'uncomplicated "tubal" patients under the age of 40, the clinical pregnancy rate (i.e. a gestation sac is visible on ultrasound) is 17 per cent per embryo replaced. In "unexplained" female infertility, the equivalent rate is 13 per cent and when male factors are present it is 8 per cent. Eleven per cent of these pregnancies abort. Not all the cycles get as far as egg recovery (although 90 per cent do), and not all the eggs fertilize, so the overall rate per cycle is much lower than the specific rates per embryo transfer given above' (personal communication, Patricia Kohn, Sheffield Fertility Centre, 11 February 1991).
5 Klinefelter's syndrome is a prenatally detectable chromosome abnormality (47XXY). One in 1,000 males has this syndrome. They are usually asymptomic during childhood with normal performance IQ scores. In adulthood, however, they are invariably infertile.

References

Aberg, A., Mitelman, F., Cantz, M. and Gehler, J. (1978) 'Cardiac puncture of fetuses with Herler's disease avoiding abortion of unaffected co-twin', *Lancet*, ii: 990.

Anderson, D.C. (1987) 'Licensing work on IVF and related procedures', *Lancet*, i: 1373.

Anonymous (1989) 'Selective feticide', *SATFA* (Support After Termination for Abnormality) *News*, 1: 3.

Berton, P. (1977) *The Dionne Years: A Thirties Melodrama*. New York: Norton.

Biggers, J.D. (1981) 'In vitro fertilization and embryo transfer in human beings', *New England Journal of Medicine*, 34: 336–42.

Botting, B., Macdonald Davies, I. and Macfarlane, A. (1987) 'Recent trends in the incidence of multiple births and associated mortality', *Archives of Diseases in Childhood*, 62: 941–50.

Botting, B., Macfarlane, A. and Price, F. (eds) (1990) *Three, Four and More: A Study of Triplets and Higher Order Births.* London: HMSO.

Brambati, B., Formigli, L., Tului, L. and Simoni, G. (1990) 'Selective reduction of quadruplet pregnancy at risk of ß-thalassaemia', *Lancet*, 336: 1325–6.

Bryan, E. (1989) 'The response of mothers to selective feticide', *Ethical Problems in Reproductive Medicine*, 1: 28–30.

Bryan, E. (1990) 'I don't want so many babies', *Multiple Births Foundation Newsletter*, 6: 3.

Contrepas, C. (1989) 'Information before pregnancy', *Multiple Births Foundation Newsletter*, 5: 2.

Derom, C., Vlietinck, R., Derom, R., Van Den Berge, H. and Thiery, M. (1987) 'Increased monozygotic twinning late after ovulation induction', *Lancet*, i: 1236–8.

Dyer, C. (1991) 'Selective reduction', *British Medical Journal*, 302: 1043.

Edwards, R.G. (1985) 'In-vitro fertilisation and embryo replacement: opening lecture', *Annuals of the New York Academy of Science*, 442: 375–80.

Edwards, R.G., Mettler, L. and Walters, D.E. (1986) 'Identical twins and in-vitro fertilisation', *Journal of In-Vitro Fertilisation and Embryo Transfer*, 3: 114–17.

Hellin, D. (1895) 'Die Ursache der Multiparitat der Unipaeren', *Tiere Uberhaupt und der Zwillingssch wangerschaft beim Menscherv Insbesondere*. Munich: Sellz and Schaner.

ILA (1990) *The Fifth Report of the Interim Licensing Authority for Human In Vitro Fertilization and Embryology*. London: ILA.

ILA (1991) *The Sixth Report of the Interim Licensing Authority for Human In Vitro Fertilization and Embryology*. London: ILA.

Kanhai, H.H.H., Van Rijssel, E.J.C., Meerman, R.J., Bennenbroek Gracenhorst, J. (1986) 'Selective terminations in quintuplet pregnancy during first trimester', *Lancet*, i: 1447.

Kennedy, I. (1988) 'What is a medical decision?', in I. Kennedy, *Treat Me Right: Essays in Medical Law and Ethics*. Oxford:

Clarendon Press, pp. 19–31.

Lancet (Editorial) (1988) 'Selective fetal reductions', *Lancet*, ii: 773–5.

Leiblum, S.R., Kemmann, E. and Takse, L. (1989) 'Attitudes toward multiple births'. Paper presented at the 9th International Congress of Psychosomatic Obstetrics and Gynaecology, Amsterdam, 28–31 May.

Levene, M.I. (1986) 'Grand multiple pregnancies and demand for neonatal intensive care', *Lancet*, ii: 347–8.

Levene, M.I. (1991) 'Assisted reproduction and its implications for paediatrics', *Archives of Diseases in Childhood*, 66: 1–3.

Macfarlane, A.J., Johnson, A. and Bower, P. (1990a) 'Disabilities and health problems in childhood', in B.J. Botting, A.J. Macfarlane and F.V. Price (eds), *Three, Four and More: A Study of Triplets and Higher Order Births*. London: HMSO, pp. 153–60.

Macfarlane, A.J., Johnson, A. and Daw, E.G. (1990b) 'The delivery', in B.J. Botting, A.J. Macfarlane and F.V. Price (eds), *Three, Four and More: A Study of Triplets and Higher Order Births*. London: HMSO, pp. 80–98.

MRC (1990) 'Births in Great Britain resulting from assisted conception, 1978–87', Working Party on Children Conceived by *In Vitro* Fertilisation, *British Medical Journal*, 300: 1229–33.

Mugford, M. (1990) 'The cost of a multiple birth', in B.J. Botting, A.J. Macfarlane and F.V. Price (eds), *Three, Four and More: A Study of Triplets and Higher Order Births*. London: HMSO, pp. 205–17.

Murray, M. and Osmond-Clark, F. (1971) 'Pregnancy results following treatment with clomiphene citrate', *Journal of Obstetrics and Gynaecology British Commonwealth*, 78: 1108.

National Perinatal Statistics Unit (1990) *IVF and GIFT Pregnancies: Australia and New Zealand 1988*. Sydney: National Perinatal Statistics Unit.

Peters, H., Nervell, S.J. and Obhrai, M. (1991) 'Impact of assisted reproduction on neonatal care', *Lancet*, 337: 797.

Price, F.V. (1990a) 'Who helps?', in B.J. Botting, A.J. Macfarlane and F.V. Price (eds), *Three, Four and More: A Study of Triplets and Higher Order Births*. London: HMSO, pp. 131–52.

Price, F.V. (1990b) 'Consequences', in B.J. Botting, A.J. Macfarlane and F.V. Price (eds), *Three, Four and More: A Study of*

Triplets and Higher Order Births. London: HMSO, pp. 161–76.

Price, F.V. (1991) 'Isn't she coping well?', in H. Roberts (ed.), *Women's Health Matters*. London: Routledge, pp. 121–40.

Price, F.V., Moores, S., Ockwell, E. and Stokes, B. (1990) 'Schooling', in B.J. Botting, A.J. Macfarlane and F.V. Price (eds), *Three, Four and More: A Study of Triplets and Higher Order Births*. London: HMSO.

Reid, Sue (1988) *Labour of Love: The Story of the World's First Surrogate Grandmother*. London: The Bodley Head.

Rodeck, C.H., Mibastion, R.S., Abramowicz, J. and Campbell, S. (1982) 'Selective feticide of the affected twin by fetoscopic air embolism', *Prenatal Diagnosis*, 2: 189.

Schenker, J.G., Yarkoni, S. and Granat, M. (1981) 'Multiple pregnancies following induction of ovulation', *Fertility and Sterility*, 35: 105–23.

Scott-Jupp, R., Field, D.M. and Macfadyen, U. (1991) 'Multiple pregnancies resulting from assisted conception: burden on neonatal units', *British Medical Journal*, 302: 1079.

Seppala, M. (1985) 'The world collaborative report of in-vitro fertilisation and embryo replacement; current state of the art in 1984', in M. Seppala and R.G. Edwards (eds), *In Vitro Fertilisation and Embryo Transfer. Annals of the New York Academy of Science*, 442: 558–63.

Serono Laboratories (UK) Ltd (1986) 'If nature can't deliver . . .'. Pamphlet 170/0886.

Steptoe, P. (1986) 'The role of in vitro fertilization in the treatment of infertility: ethical and legal problems', *Med. Sci. Law*, 26: 82.

Steven, C. (1989) 'An agonising choice – which of your babies should die?', *Sunday Times*, 5 November, F7.

Varley, W. (1989) 'A process of elimination', *Guardian*, 28 November, p. 38.

VLA (1987) *The Second Report of the Voluntary Licensing Authority for Human 'In-Vitro' Fertilization and Embryology*. London: VLA.

Wapner, R., Davis, G., Johnson, A., Weinblatt, V.J., Fischer, R.L., Jackson, L.G., Chervenak, F.A. and McCullough, L.B. (1990) 'Selective reduction on multifetal pregnancies', *Lancet*, 335: 90–3.

Waterstone, J., Parsons, J. and Bolton, V. (1991) 'Elective

transfer of two embryos', *Lancet*, 337: 975–6.

Yovitch, J.L., Matson, P.L., Blackledge, D.G., Turner, S.R., Richardson, P.A., Yovitch, J.M. and Edirisinghe, W.R. (1988) 'The treatment of normospermic infertility by gamete intra-fallopian transfer (GIFT)', *British Journal of Obstetrics and Gynaecology*, 95: 361–6.

6

Gamete donation and the social management of genetic origins

ERICA HAIMES

Many consequences arise from the use of donated semen and eggs to enable involuntarily childless people to become parents, but one in particular provides the focus of this paper: the uncertainty of how to handle information about the resultant 'child's'[1] genetic parents (for general background see Haimes, 1988b). Currently there is a fierce debate being waged between those who favour giving the 'child' full identifying information about the genetic parents and those who, by contrast, prefer to keep the genetic parents anonymous.

In this chapter I wish to present a sociological analysis of this debate: that is, not to argue for one side or the other but to analyse the nature of the debate itself, in order to discover what its existence can tell us about other, wider aspects of society in which such a debate can exist. In referring in the title of this paper to the 'social management' of this issue, I seek to emphasize that any resolution proffered necessarily reflects and affects the way such a society thinks about individuals, parents, children and families.

Characterizing and analysing the debate

Before analysing the debate it is necessary first to clarify briefly just how extensive and complex the issue of handling genetic origins can become. It is also necessary to clarify the lines along which the debate is being conducted.

The complexity of the origins issue

It is perhaps most useful to appreciate the complexity of handling questions about origins by surveying the types of intra- and extra-familial relationships which surround the 'child' who has his or her origins in the deployment of these techniques. Robert Snowden and his colleagues (1983) devised an original nomenclature to cover the contributions made by the different parties to a child's creation. The woman's role is divided into three distinct types: the genetic mother, the carrying mother and the nurturing mother; where one woman undertakes all three roles she is described as a 'complete mother'. However, various combinations are possible: for instance, a woman could be both genetic and carrying, but not nurturing, or genetic and nurturing but not carrying (as in a commissioning mother using gestatory surrogacy) or carrying and nurturing but not genetic (as in egg donation). A similar distinction can be made in the male role: a man can be a genetic father or a nurturing father, or both. However, whilst these distinctions are complex enough (and, in fact, are not entirely satisfactory)[2] an even more complex picture emerges when they are applied to the range of possible fertilization procedures.

Table 6.1 shows how complicated it might be to describe the 'origins' of any particular 'child' resulting from these procedures. Several points should be emphasized about Table 6.1. First, it is difficult to cover all the possible combinations of procedure, parental type and third party so although it is already fairly complicated, it still presents a simplified version of the 'child's' origins; second, the table would look somewhat different if the donors or surrogates were siblings to the nurturing parents since the nurturing parents[3] would in fact then have a genetic relationship with

Table 6.1 *Family relationships created through third party conceptions*

Family created through	Child's relationship to nurturing father	Child's relationship to nurturing mother		Child's relationship to third parties	
	Genetic	Genetic	Carrying	Genetic	Carrying
Donor insemination	No	Yes	Yes	Yes	No
Egg donation	Yes	No	Yes	Yes	No
Embryo donation	No	No	Yes	Yes	No
				Yes	No
Gestatory surrogacy	Yes	Yes	No	No	Yes
Genetic surrogacy	Yes	No	No	Yes	Yes
Gestatory surrogacy, using donor semen	No	Yes	No	No	Yes[1]
				Yes	No[2]
Gestatory surrogacy, using donor egg	Yes	No	No	No	Yes[1]
				Yes	No[3]
Gestatory surrogacy, plus donor embryo	No	No	No	No	Yes[1]
				Yes	No[3]
				Yes	No[2]
Genetic surrogacy, plus donor semen	No	No	No	Yes	Yes[1]
				Yes	No[2]

[1] Surrogate.
[2] Semen donor.
[3] Egg donor.

the resultant 'child'; third, it might seem rather obvious to point out that the nurturing father can never have a carrying relationship with the 'child', but it is perhaps less obvious that the third parties if kept anonymous can never have a nurturing relationship with the 'child'; fourth, it emphasizes the power of surrogacy to make the 'child's' origins particularly complex, yet this procedure is probably the least discussed in terms of the origins debate.

The nature of the debate

The history of the debate over whom to tell what about the circumstances of the conception and birth of a person resulting from gamete donation can be divided, in the United Kingdom, into three broad periods: (i) up to the early 1980s; (ii) early to mid-1980s; (iii) from 1984 onwards, after the publication of the report of the Committee of Inquiry into Human Fertilization and Embryology (the Warnock Report, DHSS, 1984). In very general terms,[4] prior to the 1980s there was little public awareness of donor insemination and the issues arising from its use. In terms of the origins debate, most commentators assumed that the means of conception would be kept secret from the 'child'; therefore the question of giving the 'child' information about the donor's identity rarely arose. Such secrecy did not meet with full approval, however, and by the early 1980s commentators such as Snowden questioned its necessity (Snowden et al., 1983). This uneasiness about the secrecy of donor insemination was discussed by the Warnock Committee, which then recommended that the 'child' should be told about the means of his or her conception, but that the identity of the donor (whether of semen or ova) should not be revealed.

It is possible to identify three positions on the question of secrecy and gamete donation which have emerged since the publication of the Warnock Report:

1   those who still advocate keeping the means of the

conception (and therefore the identity of the donors)
secret;

2   those who argue a 'child' should be told how he or she
    was conceived but who argue the donors should remain
    anonymous;

3   those who argue a 'child' should be told about the means
    of conception and should have access, at the age of 18, to
    information about the donor's identity.

In the public, professional and parliamentary debates which
led to the Human Fertilization and Embryology Act, 1990,
the first of these positions lost ground and the origins debate
coalesced around the other two. The Act itself follows the
recommendations of the Warnock Report fairly closely on
this matter: section 31(3) allows a person conceived through
gamete donation the right to apply at the age of 18 for
information about the donor, a provision which rests of
course on the assumption that such a person would have
been told (or could somehow have discovered) his or her
means of conception. The Act does not specify what that
information should be, though the earlier White Paper
'Human Fertilization and Embryology: A Framework for
Legislation' had given some indication that it may, in fact,
be identifying (DHSS, 1987: 14). However, the Code of
Practice, published in August 1991 by the Human Fertilization and Embryology Authority (established by the 1990
Act) specified that donors should be told that 'the Act
generally permits donors to preserve their anonymity' (1991:
4iii). Even so, since the Act requires identifying information
about donors to be recorded, there is always the possibility
that in the future identifying information could be made
available to the 'children', albeit not retrospectively given
the provisions elsewhere in the Act (section 31(5)).

Outside the United Kingdom, different positions have
been taken on this issue. In Sweden, legislation passed in
1983 (Statens Offentliga Utredningar, Sweden, 1983) gives
the 'child' the right to identifying information about semen

donors; in Australia the Waller Report (1983) recommended that non-identifying information should be given to
both 'child' and donor, and that full identifying information
about donors should be stored on a central register; Walters
(1987) recounts that out of nine reports published in a range
of countries since the Warnock Report, one did not consider
the issue, four require donor anonymity and four others do
not. Rautenan (personal communication, 1990) reports that
in Finland the issue has been debated mostly between the
medical profession, who favour anonymity, and social work
professionals, who favour non-anonymity. The issue remains unresolved there. Finally, the Glover Report, produced for the European Commission, suggested that member states should adopt the Swedish model 'for an ex-
perimental period' (Glover et al., 1989: 38) but none so far
appears to have taken up this suggestion.

The origins issue is still therefore very open-ended,
leaving those with firm views with much to play for, both in
the United Kingdom and elsewhere. Certainly, in the UK
the debate is still being fiercely waged. As in Finland, one
aspect of the debate has been the divide between clinical and
social work professionals. Two recent publications exem-
plify clearly just what the issues are and the terms in which
the debate has been and is still being conducted. The first, a
book published by the British Agencies for Adoption and
Fostering (Walby and Symons, 1990) argues for the removal
of donor anonymity on the following grounds.

1 The procedures of gamete donation can benefit from the
   experience of adoption which has demonstrated that
   knowledge about genetic heritage is important for a
   person to develop a clear sense of identity; therefore
   such people have 'a right and a need' (1990: 110) to be
   told who their genetic parents are.
2 The Warnock Report and policy statements since have
   failed to appreciate the first point because they neglect
   the interests of the person created by gamete donation in

favour of the alleged parental wish for privacy.

3   Secrecy about such matters will 'cast a shadow and create a tension in the family which is likely to be detrimental to all' (1990: 113) though it is also acknowledged that parents might need help in conveying such information to their 'children'.

The contrary view expressed in the *British Medical Journal* by Braude et al. (1990) argues for the retention of donor anonymity on the following grounds.

1   There is a lack of evidence to support the claim that it is in the 'child's' interests to have access to information about his or her genetic parents; figures for the number of adoptees who search for similar information indicate a lack of interest in these matters.

2   Donors wish to remain anonymous and will cease to donate if anonymity is not guaranteed; support for this is claimed from Sweden where the law allowing the identification of donors is said to have led to a dramatic reduction in the donor population.

3   It is not possible to establish paternity[5] clearly, other than by genetic fingerprinting, yet there is a variety of circumstances when, despite the use of donor sperm, the donor may not be the 'child's' genetic father; to use genetic fingerprinting would, however, lead to a more widespread testing of paternity which 'would be very destructive to the family' (1990: 1411).

Analysing the debate

Both these viewpoints have their strengths and weaknesses.[6] Walby and Symons's arguments (1990) try to ensure full consideration is given to all parties involved in these procedures, including the 'child'; too often the focus is on the needs of the infertile couple, to the neglect of the interests of the person being created. Also they write with the experience of those with a detailed involvement in families who have had to deal with similar problems, such as in adoption and fostering. They convey the complexity of family interaction with a clarity which suggests an understanding of the gradual accumulation of potential difficulties. However, there is a danger that they invest too great a significance in the notion of the 'blood tie' without clarifying exactly how that relates to the complex notion of 'identity' (see Haimes, 1987; Humphrey and Humphrey, 1986; O'Donovan, 1989). Equally, they have a tendency to overstate the position in adoption, since a detailed analysis of practice and legislation in that area suggests that full openness does not yet exist (see Haimes, 1988a).

The arguments of Braude et al. can be evaluated in the same manner. As I suggest above they are right to question the nature of the comparison with adoption and to demand greater clarity about claims based on the 'need to know' argument. Equally, it is important to point out, as they do, the difficulties of ensuring that full and accurate information is recorded by all parties.

However, there are also serious errors of fact and other weaknesses in this article. First, in criticizing the adoption parallel the authors misrepresent the legislation on access to birth records in adoption; they also give the figure 5 per cent as the level of interest in access to adoption records without acknowledging the difficulties of arriving at this or any other measure of the level of interest. Secondly, much of their argument rests on the assertion that donors wish to remain anonymous but the empirical research evidence indicates a much greater willingness by donors to be named than is often presumed (Bruce, 1990; Daniels, 1988; Morgan and Lee, 1991: 163; Rowland, 1985). Thirdly, the claim that the number of donors in Sweden has fallen has been strongly contested by McWhinnie (1990) and by Stjerna (personal communication, 1990).

There are other points of detail and theoretical interest which can be made about both sides of this argument, but the points raised here are already sufficient to indicate that it is difficult to arbitrate between the two positions. The question then becomes one of how to make progress in the debate, to break the stalemate. I suggest this has to be done by taking the analysis one step further, to establish the grounds on which the debate as a whole, rather than one side or the other, rests, since, for the sociologist, there is the awareness that for the debate even to exist in the first place, each side must have certain cultural assumptions in common. It is already clear, for example, that the opposing sides do share some concerns, such as seeing 'the family' as somehow important, though exactly how is not always clear. This suggests that the debate is linked to wider concerns, which tend, however, to remain unstated, given the narrowness of the parameters within which the debate tends actually to be conducted. Therefore it is necessary to try to prise open those unstated assumptions upon which the debate rests, to see what process of reasoning, and what repertoire of concerns, are available to those participating in such discussions.[7]

One example of just such an attempt may be found in a piece of research I conducted with members of the Warnock Committee, which was directed towards discovering, in greater depth, how and why certain policies on the management of genetic origins were arrived at, to see if the results of such an investigation help to shed light on the debate itself. I decided in this research to concentrate on the work of the Warnock Committee for several reasons.

1 The committee represents the most influential attempt in the UK to manage the issue of genetic origins.
2 The members of the committee were part of, and in turn helped to create, the structures by which certain facts about the origins of people created through gamete donation are rendered knowable and certain facts rendered unknowable. Therefore, by investigating what, for them, were the important factors it should be possible to start to identify the repertoire of considerations which

they brought to their task, thus shedding a little more light on the complexities of the origins issues and the basis to the whole debate.

3   The recommendation of the Warnock Committee which, to recap, was to tell the 'child' about the means of conception but not to identify the donors, represents a middle position between those who advocate complete secrecy about the means of conception (and also therefore about the donor's identity) and those who advocate complete openness about both the means of conception and the identity of the donor(s). Therefore it is particularly interesting to see how they picked their way through these difficult and controversial questions, to arrive at what could be seen, retrospectively at least, as a position of compromise.

Therefore, through a detailed analysis of their final report and through the analysis of indepth interviews[8] which provide an explicit display of both the puzzles which confronted the Committee and the way they reasoned through those puzzles, I tried to establish and analyse their reasons for managing the genetic origins issue in this way.

Research findings

From the interviews, two distinctive positions were evident on the question of managing origins information: those members who were *firmly* in favour of anonymity and those who were, *on balance*, in favour of anonymity. The majority of members appear to be in the second group but nobody advocated naming donors as a matter of policy.

Members' reasons for being strongly in favour of anonymity varied. One said to identify donors

is probably socially not acceptable because it's a much less personal thing than actually giving an adopted child the right to ascertain the identity of his or her natural parents because that child was actually born to another couple.

But this is simply, as I say, a donation of a single cell if you like and it doesn't seem to me to be appropriate or in the interests of preserving the anonymity of the donors that the child should be allowed actually to know who the donor was because after all they've been paid, it's just purely a commercial transaction as far as they're concerned.

Another member asserted that it was 'absolutely essential' to preserve the anonymity of donation since it would be 'shattering' for the donor if the 'child' turned up. He also questioned whether it was really in the 'child's' interests to confront someone who had 'masturbated off' as a donor. The impression held by these speakers therefore is of donation, specifically of semen, as being a limited act which would be of no benefit either to donor or 'child' to develop further, into any other sort of relationship. Those who 'on balance' were in favour of anonymity were weighing up the various different difficulties which could occur were anonymity to be removed. There was also the weight of history in the practice of donor insemination to be considered:

> I think behind the fact that we favoured anonymity was that this was the status quo and it just happened to be the way that early practitioners in AID did it. They did it that way probably because they had to be rather furtive about it . . . I think I was also concerned for other reasons, not just the status quo, but also because we did feel, or I felt, that the problem of emotional entanglements loomed as soon as you removed anonymity.

This speaker cited as an example of such entanglements the image of the 'child' discovering 'its aunt was its mother, that sort of thing'.

Members had an idea of the benefits to be derived from anonymity though these were expressed mostly in terms of the benefits to the recipients and their families, and to donors and their families, rather than the 'child'. In terms of the recipients one member reasoned,

> From the point of view of a third party intervention in a
> marriage which you mentioned earlier as one of the big
> concerns about gamete donation then I would think
> anonymity goes a long way to meet that, because as long
> as the donor is anonymous I think the couple very soon
> ceases to think of it as a third party being involved in the
> marriage and the relationship. If the donor has a name
> and address and a profession and an image, if they'd met
> him or her, then it would be much more a real person, a
> real third person intruding in their marriage. I think that
> would make it more difficult. So I think many recipients
> would prefer to maintain anonymity.

There were some very strong concerns expressed about
the effect on the donor if anonymity were removed. Some
members cited the fear that the supply of donors would
disappear while another suggested 'he' had the right to 'fade
out of the scene' since donation means giving without
strings, rights or obligations. Certainly the issue of paternal
liability[9] was raised as a reason for maintaining anonymity:
'I don't personally feel these difficulties very strongly, but I
do think that as long as the law is as it is now there would be
a threat to the donor if the children turned up on his
doorstep.'

The ramifications for the donor's family were important.
One member argued that quite a lot of wives do not want
their husbands to be donors, 'they just don't like the idea of
him producing other children'. This though is an objection
to the fact of donation not to the identification of the donor.
Another member created this image: 'What havoc . . . on
the front doorstep, the advent of this other member of your
husband's family, no connection with you at all, no
connection with your own family, except through the father.
It would create such dreadful upheavals in the families . . .'.
These are the same graphic devices for expressing the fears
associated with tracing genetic parents in adoption. The

family as here, or just to the individual donor as earlier, produces the same overall effect of the intruding individual, outside, on the doorstep, threatening the inside world of the family home. Anonymity it would seem has as much to do with protecting the donor's family from intrusion by the 'child' as it has to do with protecting the nurturing family from the donor.

While they were concerned to protect families, members appeared to be less clear about the 'child's' position with regard to donor anonymity. There was little doubt that the 'child' should know about his or her conception, but about the 'child's' right or interest in knowing who the donor was, one member said, 'I don't know about that, I'm awfully sorry, I just can't comment on it.' His view was that some would need to know, others would not, but he did not feel there should be access to this information anyway. Another member agreed that a lot would depend on the individual 'child', though he had no doubt about the state's right to withhold the information, especially if it considered that to be in the 'child's' best interests: it could always change later if the evidence suggested that it should. Overall though, 'I find your question exceedingly difficult to comment on.'

Other members expressed their uncertainty about the 'child's' position:

I'm not certain in my own mind how much this 'need to know' about your *own* parents is really a burning need. So I'm really uncertain about this. As I say, I'm willing to be convinced [pause]. There are some things in life we can't have, can't do, say for instance not being able to have children. It comes in a way in the same category, not being able to transmit a bit of yourself into the future, . . . so I feel sorry for people who haven't got children and aren't able to do that when they want to. In the same way perhaps some people have to face the fact they can't find out about their parentage. You know, I'm not certain that everyone has an inalienable right, or a need, to do it. I mean I think we talk too glibly about everybody needing to know.

The presumption here is that withholding the information would be the starting point and that a case would have to be made for gaining access to the information, rather than for continuing to withhold it. The parallel raised with infertile adults is interesting, though it raises as many questions as it answers, especially as it might be argued that the two cases are not parallels, but rather that one is the consequence of the other. That is, the process of helping infertile people to have children actively creates the situation in which those 'children' might then have their genetic origins rendered unknowable.

Two members explicitly weighed the 'child's' potential wish for information against the wishes of the families involved. One said it was in the interests of the receiving family, on balance, that the 'child' should know nothing about the donor. Another member who has already been quoted about her concerns for the donor's family if a 'child' turns up, generalized this point at a later stage:

> I'm very concerned about the effect of complete laying on the table of personal details of name and age and photographs and all the rest of it, the effect that that would have on families. I think at the risk . . . of upsetting one person who wants to know rather more than is available for that person to know and upsetting *complete* families, I think the balance is too great, on one side.

This further emphasizes the importance attributed to 'complete families' against the wishes of the individual.

Members though were not insensitive to the 'child's' position: 'Oh yes, I mean, in a funny way it's not very nice that a doctor knows who your true father is and you don't or that the doctor knows who your carrying mother was and you don't.' They felt mostly, however, that it was still better to stick to non-identifying information.

The difficulty of handling genetic origins was summed up by one member who said he wracked his brains over the question of anonymity and argued that although the committee favoured anonymity it was possible to see contrary arguments 'peeking out' from one or two paragraphs in the report. 'I think all the committee felt that anonymity was not an open and shut case . . . I think frankly, if the whole practice of AID had started on a non-anonymous basis then we would have just probably have accepted that one too.' This tends to make the use of secrecy and anonymity sound as though it was an accident of history, but as I have noted elsewhere (Haimes, 1990b), earlier practitioners and committees and commentators had reasons for favouring anonymity (mostly to do with disguising the use of donor insemination in which donor anonymity was a constituent element of a much wider practice of secrecy) just as members of the Warnock Committee had their reasons for not changing that situation completely.

One final view was that these issues had to be seen within the context of society, which this member saw as being in a 'very flexible febrile state' about this sort of thing. He proffered a solution which would have the effect of attaching the 'child', emotionally, to the nurturing family:

I think in the final analysis the ability of the child in most cases to respond to and cope with these strange revelations is to do with the emotional warmth and stability in which the family setting, one parent or two parents, offers the child and that that more than anything else is determinative. If that isn't there you're going to have problems anyhow. So I find this a very grey area where I've listened to a lot of evidence and read a lot of arguments but where I think you don't come down very clearly, where there are advantages on both sides of the argument. Where I think that, granted I can't easily choose between these sides, I'll say whichever method you're using should be consistent.

He concluded, however, that since it was difficult to go back on a confidence revealed, the onus was on the new, open, procedure

> to show that it will flourish better from non-anonymity than anonymity. Until such time the state has no alternative but to take a decision which . . . it believes will suit the majority. It knows that it won't suit everybody and that's the sort of painful decision the state has to take.

In many ways this is a useful summary of the Warnock Committee's position though in fact this member was referring to the state in a wider sense. It also demonstrates, once again, that the starting point for discussions was anonymity, rather than a position which asked why anonymity specifically existed in the first place.

Shared grounds?

The interviews with members of the Warnock Committee provide further insight into what are taken to be relevant considerations for those participating in the management of the origins issue. If those data are combined with the arguments put forward by Walby and Symons (1990) on the one hand, and by Braude et al. (1990) on the other, we can begin to see the grounds on which this debate and the origins issue as a whole, rest. Grounds which are, of course, common to all those entering the debate, from whatever position. There are at least five areas of commonality.

1   It is noticeable that there is a lack of information about the people who have been conceived by donated gametes, even though semen donation has been widely used since the 1940s. Thus both sides of the debate, and others, have to use explanations derived from elsewhere, that is, adoption, which is taken to raise similar issues. Whether that is the case or not (and I have argued elsewhere that we need to be

cautious about making this assumption; see Haimes, 1988a), it should be noted that this lack of information derives from the practice of keeping the use of donor insemination secret since the 1940s.

2   The issue is approached by taking anonymity as the starting point. Those who are anti-anonymity feel they have to make a case for changing current practices and attitudes in the light of experience from elsewhere and those who are pro-anonymity tend to conduct the argument in terms of a response to these calls, rather than from first principles. This is also evident in that final quotation from the Warnock Committee member. Nowhere is the debate conducted in terms of asking why, in a society which routinely provides information about genetic origins, for example, in the form of open access to birth certificates,[10] an exception has been made for those people not being raised by their genetic parents. It should be possible to ask why, for them, that information has been rendered unknowable in the first place. This raises different issues from those raised by justifying why anonymity should be continued, once it has been established. This is a point I shall return to later.

3   We can see both in how the Warnock Committee members puzzled over this question and in the way Walby and Symons (1990), on the one hand, and Braude et al. (1990) on the other, argue for their particular points that there is a certain degree of puzzlement about the importance of genetic ties (and biological factors in general) in family life. In resolving these puzzles the two sides of the debate employ contradictory notions about the importance of genetic relationships, both to the individual and to the family. For example, those who are anti-anonymity recommend openness about genetic origins, on the grounds that it is the quality of the social relationships that is important in constituting 'the family', rather than the fact that family members are genetically tied to each other. The quality of

the social relationships is measured by the degree of willingness of the nurturing parents to be open with the 'child'. However, in asserting the need for an individual to know his or her genetic origins they are, at the same time, making a claim about the fundamental role of biology in constituting that individual. The question of how that which they consider important in constituting the individual (biology/genetics) should be reconciled with that which they consider important in constituting the family (social relationships) is not addressed.

Similarly, those who are pro-anonymity recommend secrecy about the identity of the genetic parents on the grounds that it is not clear how important such information is to the person conceived. This entails, therefore, denying its importance. Indeed that could be the case for allowing gamete donation in the first place on the grounds that (and here they move very close to those who are anti-anonymity) the source of the genetic material for actually creating the 'child' is unimportant to a 'real' family, since what counts there is the quality of the social relationships in building a family life together. However, there is a contradiction in this position too since genetic ties are clearly, from their other arguments, *not* unimportant since, if they were, there would be nothing to fear from their being exposed and therefore no need for anonymity between donor and child. Therefore, is it merely a 'commercial transaction' as one Warnock Committee member asserted?

The sheer fact of wanting to preserve elaborate devices for retaining anonymity is an indication that the genetic tie is actually regarded as very important indeed, such that the consequences of the discovery of a genetic tie outwith the family (for donor as well as child) are considered so serious that they must be guarded against. Anonymity implies that the existence of a genetic tie between donor and 'child' would exert some sort of 'pull' (Achilles, 1986) between the two which, if responded to, would be disruptive to both families. Therefore the pro-anonymity stance also attributes some sort of fundamental nature to the 'genetic tie' (note the phrase itself) though at the same time denying its importance.

4 All participants in the debate are also undoubtedly concerned about 'the family'[11] as it affects and is affected by these issues. One aspect in particular causes much difficulty: how to weigh the interests of one individual against those of another in the family since each side in fact has to *prioritize* the claims of one individual within the family over the claims of others. That is, those who are pro-anonymity prioritize the needs of the nurturing parents for privacy about the details of their infertility and, as one of the members argued, the privacy of their marriage, over the 'child's' needs for information about the donor; those who are anti-anonymity reverse these priorities. (Similarly, prioritization has to occur between the 'child's' needs and the donor's needs.)

5 There appears, however, to be some uneasiness about ranking claims in this way when each side of the debate also feels a need to make some assertions, as we have seen, about the quality of the family's life as a whole. Hence both sides, while basing their arguments on the ranking of one individual's claims over another's, none the less couch the merits of their case in terms of the benefits to be gained by the family as a whole. The quality of family life is seen to be enhanced by openness on the one side and anonymity on the other. That is, these merits are seen to justify the claims made on behalf of any particular individual (parent or child, and, at one remove the donor, whose family is also thought to benefit from anonymity as is particularly clear from the Warnock Committee interviews). Advocates of both sides of the argument appear to feel that their case will be more readily accepted by the audience to which they are addressing their views, and will therefore carry greater weight if those views are couched in terms of benefits to the family.

It should be noted, however, that these families are perceived by both sides of the debate as discrete, exclusive, self-contained units, such that fathers and mothers can only be 'real' fathers and mothers in *one* family and, similarly, 'children' can only be 'real' children in *one* family. For both sides of the debate the nurturing parents appear to be considered the 'real' parents, not just in the 'child's' family, but also interestingly in the donor's family (for example, the semen donor is regarded as 'really' the father of the children he raises, not a father of the 'child' conceived from his donation). Thus, while the donor could be regarded as a potential intruder on the 'child's' family, equally the 'child' can be regarded as a potential intruder on the donor's family (expressed graphically in the reference by one of the Warnock Committee to 'havoc on the doorstep'). The only difference between the two sides of the debate is their choice of strategy in dealing with this possibility: by making all information available, so that the 'child' can decide whom he or she regards as his or her 'real' parents (with the expectation that this will be the nurturing parents)[12] or by preventing the possibility in the first place, through the mechanism of anonymity. Therefore, whatever position is taken on the importance attributed to the 'genetic tie' (see point 2 above), much of the debate is implicitly directed towards establishing the authenticity of particular family units and, as a consequence, the discrete boundaries of those units.

As is often the case, therefore, two sides virulently opposed to each other in an argument actually have much more in common than might first be supposed and it is these areas of common ground which make the debate possible. They demonstrate what is considered thinkable and relevant when discussing these issues and, as a consequence, they tell us something about the broader aspects of the society in which such a debate occurs.

Conclusions: what are the lessons?

I think we learn two inter-related sets of lessons from investigating this debate and identifying these common grounds. The first set concerns the practical resolution of the debate itself, the second set concerns the theoretical (and hence more widely relevant) connections between the debate and what it indicates about this society.

Practical lessons: resolving the debate

Having identified how close in fact the two sides of the argument are, the question then becomes how, practically, either side can break the apparent stalemate. There would appear to be three possibilities. First, one or the other side could prove beyond reasonable doubt that the policies of the opposite side are so damaging that they cannot, morally, be sustained. This, however, is the least likely solution since it would require greater precision over terminology, a comparative trial of all the possible effects and a measurable notion of 'damage', all of which would be exceedingly difficult to achieve.

The second position is for one or other side to resolve the contradictions which I have identified here as lying behind both arguments concerning the importance attributed to biological and social factors in constituting the family. The logic of consistency would then allow that side to carry greater weight. Whether it is in fact possible for either side to do this seems doubtful since, as I have shown, those contradictions lie at the heart of each side of the debate. However, as a strategy this would probably marginally favour those who are pro-anonymity since the very nature of controlling information and promoting forms of secrecy would at least help to conceal the existence of the contradiction even if it cannot remove it.

A third possibility, however, would be to shift the grounds of one or other side of the debate such that there were two much more *distinctive* sets of claims being made (rather than just the *appearance* of distinctive claims). This might tend to favour those who are anti-anonymity since it is possible to argue this case on the grounds of civil liberties, or a more general notion of 'freedom of information'. Elements of such an argument are developing. For example, Morgan and Lee (1991: 162) cite an earlier judgment which drew on the declaration of the European Convention on Human Rights. This requires that 'everyone should be able to establish details of their identity as individual human beings'. Similarly, Bruce (1990) cites Articles 7 and 8 of the United Nations Convention on the Rights of the Child of 1989 which argue for the right of a child to a name, a nationality, knowledge of his or her parents and the right to preserve his or her identity. Since these rights are tied to notions of identity, however, they do not yet go beyond the earlier arguments of Walby and Symons (1990), in so far as the link between identity and knowledge of genetic parentage is still being asserted rather than explicated. If the language of rights replaces that of needs, however, at least two things happen: first, a social dimension replaces the individualized claims of (at least in this context) 'psychological' needs; second, the idea that an exception is being made for this particular group of people is removed and is replaced instead by the idea that they are simply being brought in line with the rights enjoyed, in a much more routine manner, by most others in society.[13]

In other words, this sort of shift in grounds would remind us that in most Western societies, interest in 'origins' (however defined) and in families is a cultural norm, being one of the ways through which we socially place ourselves and others (see Harris, 1983). Although there is variation in how that interest is expressed (for example, from government policies on the family to the congratulations offered to new parents, to, indeed, the theme of the family which has run through this chapter hitherto) there is no general surprise that such interest is expressed. Therefore, *any* individual's interest in his or her family, or 'the family' in general, is a reflection of, and constitutive of, those cultural norms and values.

Following on from this it could be argued that the actual or potential expression of interest in origins information by a person conceived through third party donations is not exceptional and is not therefore inherently problematic. It is how that interest is then managed which problematizes it. This would not automatically win the case for naming donors, but would change the emphasis from seeing interest in origins as problematic or as an exceptional demand which has to be justified (or denied), to one where the *problematization* of such interests has to be justified (and where consequently the anonymity of donors has to be justified and argued from first principles).[14]

Changing the language of the debate thus demands a much clearer, contemporary reasoning for the fact that a major exception is being made regarding routine access to information[15] against a group of people who, by definition, could not be consulted about a procedure, in favour of other groups of people (donors, the infertile) who had real choices about their involvement. This would be my own position on this debate since it would be the logical outcome of my earlier point about asking why information on genetic origins has been rendered unknowable in the first place.

Theoretical lessons: making the connections

However, the fact that anonymity *is* the starting point for these debates and that this is tied also to the other points which the two sides have in common, tells us a great deal about the issue of genetic origins and how it is linked to ideas about the family and hence to ideas about the organization of society. What is most clear is that however much either side wants to defend the creation of families through the use of gametes from outside that family, their way of managing that creation indicates a more fundamental position which suggests they see such families as actually very odd in some way. Even those who argue against anonymity do so on the grounds that previous experiences with other families of similar composition tell us that in fact those families are all right if handled in a particular way: this is an argument though which presumes the acceptance of the underlying principle that initially caution must be exercised with such families. Caution because they are 'different' in some way. However, the notion of 'difference' depends on the corollary notion of 'normal'. What we are being told by those debating the management of information on genetic origins is that there is a norm to which all families should conform and if that norm is not achieved then supplementary strategies must be devised to handle the consequences. Where that leaves us, however, is asking what the requirements of normality are. Yet it is very clear from the earlier discussions about whether 'real' families are socially or biologically constructed that this is in fact a very slippery concept, even though it is used unquestioningly by both sides of the debate. If, however, the third position outlined above for resolving the debate were adopted, one outcome might be that opposition to anonymity might take a different form from that outlined in this debate. It could, for example, concentrate on establishing the legitimacy of a range of family forms and would certainly avoid the need to defend the authenticity of *particular* types of family relationships and family units. This would avoid the weaknesses of an argument based on the individualized and imprecise concepts of 'identity needs' and at the same time would lead to a disintegration of concepts of 'normality' as applied to families, motherhood and fatherhood. This would, of course, then have its own social consequences, which would in turn be open to empirical and theoretical investigations by future social scientists.

Each of these points about the relationship between anonymity of donors and ideas about the family can be subjected to a more detailed analysis, which I have conducted elsewhere (Haimes, 1990a, 1990b). For the moment, however, my purpose is simply to illustrate that the handling of genetic origins is not a simple matter, but can be shown, through a sociological analysis, to have consequences for and connections to other aspects of the wider society.

Notes

I should like to acknowledge, with thanks, the assistance of Peter Morris, Frances Price, Peter Selman, Meg Stacey, Marilyn Strathern and Robin Williams.

1 I shall be using the term 'child' for the sake of clarity when describing the person conceived through third party donations but it should be noted that this phrase if used indiscriminately tends to mean that those people are always seen as 'children' and their views as adults are frequently neglected or negated as a result.

2 These categories, like any other, have to be understood in terms of their social context. Snowden's work was among the earliest to attempt such a classification system, when little was being written about the new reproductive technologies, especially from a sociological perspective. However, even though this topic is now firmly on the social science, as well as the public, agenda, no single classificatory system of parenting roles has gained dominance – which itself is a feature of the issues addressed in this chapter. Even the Human Fertilization and Embryology Act, 1990, which only attempted narrow, legal definitions of motherhood and fatherhood found itself in some difficulty and managed to create the category of 'legally fatherless' child (Morgan and Lee, 1991: 155). I have therefore used Snowden's terms as a short-cut to introducing the complexity of the origins issue, rather than as a full endorsement of the terms themselves. The notion of the 'complete' mother or father is particularly contentious. I address these issues at greater length in Haimes (1990b: ch. 1).

3 Although I have used 'parents' here it is clearly technically possible from these procedures to have only one nurturing parent. However, the Human Fertilization and Embryology Act, 1990 encourages the view that these procedures should only be available to couples. Since there is not enough room here to analyse these issues at length I refer the reader to Haimes (1990a, 1990b).

4 Again, more detail on the historical and international dimensions to this topic may be found in Haimes (1990b: ch. 2).

5 There is a tendency, displayed here by Braude et al. (1990) but evident elsewhere too, to narrow discussions down from a consideration of third party conceptions, to gamete donation to semen donation.

6 Other points have been raised on both sides of the debate and have been analysed in Haimes (1990b: ch. 3), but rather than discuss the debate in general terms I prefer here to take specific examples to demonstrate more clearly and precisely how certain ideas are deployed in the construction of a case either for or against donor anonymity.

7 Which also illustrates part of what is meant by 'doing sociology' (see Chapter 1): not dealing with matters as isolated issues but showing how they are linked to broader aspects of society.

8 Out of a potential 17 interviews (16 members plus secretary) I was able to conduct 14 interviews and I corresponded with a fifteenth person. The interviews were conducted in May and June 1988. Thirteen were taped and fully transcribed.

9 Though a legitimate concern in general, other provisions in the Warnock Report were directed towards removing paternal or maternal liabilities on donors, which means that in this instance such a concern is misplaced. It is interesting to note, however, that section 44 of the Human Fertilization and Embryology Act, 1990 provides for the possibility of a person born disabled as a result of a donated gamete to sue the donor for damages. This though clearly cannot be used as grounds for keeping donors anonymous and indeed may, under the 1990 Act, create one small category of such persons who may gain access to the donor's identity (see Morgan and Lee, 1991: 174-7).

10 It could be argued that such information is not routinely made available to all 'children', e.g. those conceived either through an adulterous relationship or through a non-marital relationship, in which the genetic father's identity is not recorded on the birth certificate. Two points have to be made to clarify the distinction between these cases and the one being discussed here: first, neither of these two other examples is recognized, approved nor regulated by the state in quite the way that third party conceptions are; second, and possibly as a consequence of this first point, in neither of these two other examples has a strong case been made by the state that the 'child' be told of how he or she was conceived. In other words, gamete donation at the very least (surrogacy is less clear here admittedly) has received the approval of the state but is then handled differently by the state in terms of provisions made for access to birth certificates and/or genetic parentage information. It is in this sense that an exception is being made regarding the routine provision of information about genetic origins.

11 I am not here trying to judge the 'genuine' nature of this concern. It

could be argued that clinicians are as, or more, concerned to preserve their practice of gamete donation and believe they have to advocate donor anonymity, and its benefits to the family, to do so. Similarly, social work professionals might be concerned to establish their authority and expertise in a field hitherto dominated by clinicians. What is important, however, is that it is seen as wholly appropriate either to tie their other concerns to that of the family or indeed to disguise those concerns as expressions of family interests. The question then becomes how they construct that appropriateness and what are the consequences of their so doing?

12 It can be seen for example that in much adoption literature, especially that which favours telling adoptees full details about their origins (e.g. Triseliotis, 1973) there is what has been termed a 'literature of reassurance' (Haimes and Timms, 1983: 118) which comforts adoptive parents with the view that even adoptees who trace their biological parents still regard their adoptive parents as their 'real' parents.

13 A version of this approach could be to argue that the child's rights not only exist but are the paramount consideration. However, the Code of Practice published by the Human Fertilization and Embryology Authority states explicitly that, in considering the wishes and needs of those people seeking treatment and of any children involved 'neither consideration is paramount over the other' (1991: 3i).

14 In so far as the Glover Report suggests that the 'child's' interests create 'a strong presumption in favour of openness' (Glover et al., 1989) it might be thought that this is close to the line I suggest here. However, that report still takes anonymity as the starting point and sees it as a position of safety to retreat to, should the experiment of naming donors not be successful.

15 See note 10 above.

References

Achilles, R.G. (1986) 'The social meanings of biological ties'. Doctoral thesis, University of Toronto, Canada.

Braude, P., Johnson, M. and Aitken, R.J. (1990) 'Human Fertilization and Embryology Bill goes to report stage', *British Medical Journal*, 300: 1410–2.

Bruce, N. (1990) 'On the importance of genetic knowledge', *Children and Society*, 4(2): 183–96.

Daniels, K. (1988) 'Artificial insemination using donor semen and the issue of secrecy', *Social Science and Medicine*, 27(4): 377–83.

Department of Health and Social Security (1984) *Report of the Committee of Inquiry into Human Fertilization and Embryology* ('Warnock Report'). Cmnd 9314. London: HMSO.

Department of Health and Social Security (1987) *Human Fertilization and Embryology: a Framework for Legislation* ('White Paper'). London: HMSO.

Glover, J., et. al. (1989) *Fertility and the Family*. The Glover Report on Reproductive Technologies to the European Commission. London: Fourth Estate.

Haimes, E. (1987) '"Now I know who I really am". Identity change and redefinitions of the self in adoption', in T. Honess and K. Yardley (eds), *Self and Identity*. London: Routledge and Kegal Paul, pp. 359–71.

Haimes, E. (1988a) 'Secrecy: what can artificial reproduction learn from adoption?', *International Journal of Law and the Family*, 2: 46–61.

Haimes, E. (1988b) 'Is genetic knowledge important? A sociological analysis', in N. Bruce, A. Mitchell and K. Priestley (eds), *Truth and the Child*. Edinburgh: Family Care, pp. 31–4.

Haimes, E. (1990a) 'Recreating the family?' in M. McNeil, I. Varcoe and S. Yearley (eds), *The New Reproductive Technologies*. Basingstoke: Macmillan.

Haimes, E. (1990b) 'Family connections: the management of biological origins in the new reproductive technologies'. Doctoral thesis, Department of Social Policy, University of Newcastle, pp. 154–72.

Haimes, E. and Timms, N. (1983) 'Access to birth records and counselling of adopted persons under Section 26 of the Children Act, 1975'. Final Report to the Department of Health and Social Security. London: DHSS.

Harris, C. (1983) *The Family and Industrial Society*. London: Allen and Unwin.

Human Fertilization and Embryology Authority (1991) *Code of Practice*. London: HFEA.

Humphrey, M. and Humphrey, H. (1986) 'A fresh look at genealogical bewilderment', *British Journal of Medical Psychology*, 59: 133–40.

McWhinnie, A. (1990) *A Report on Artificial Insemination*

Practices and Policies in Sweden. Dundee: University of Dundee.

Morgan, D. and Lee, R. (1991) *Blackstone's Guide to the Human Fertilization and Embryology Act, 1990.* London: Blackstone Press.

O'Donovan, K. (1989) 'What shall we tell the children?', in R. Lee and D. Morgan (eds), *Birthrights.* London: Routledge and Kegan Paul, pp. 96–114.

Rowland, R. (1985) 'The social and psychological consequences of secrecy in AID programmes', *Social Science and Medicine,* 21(4): 391–6.

Snowden, R., Mitchell, G.D. and Snowden, E. (1983) *Artificial Reproduction.* London: Allen and Unwin.

Statens Offentliga Utredningar, Sweden (1983) 'Children conceived by artificial insemination'. Stockholm: SOU, p. 42.

Triseliotis, J. (1973) *In Search of Origins.* London: Routledge and Kegan Paul.

Walby, C. and Symons, B. (1990) *Who am I? Identity, Adoption and Human Fertilization.* London: British Agencies for Adoption and Fostering.

Waller Report (1983) *Committee to Consider the Social, Ethical and Legal Issues Arising from In Vitro Fertilization: Report on Donor Gametes in In Vitro Fertilization.* Government of Victoria, Australia.

Walters, L. (1987) 'Ethics and the new reproductive technologies', *Hastings Center Report Special Supplement,* 17(5), pp. 1–5.

7

The meaning of assisted kinship

MARILYN STRATHERN

At the 1987 meetings of the British Association for the Advancement of Science, a speaker in the Psychology section asked why the concept of kinship in human beings was a problem. Pamela Wells was commenting on the way non-human animals modify their behaviour on the basis of relatedness to other members of their species. Tadpoles can apparently tell the difference between siblings, half-siblings and unrelated individuals, while some bees behave as though they can distinguish 14 degrees of relatedness. Human beings have similar facilities: mothers are able to distinguish their own infant from others by cry within 48 hours of birth, and by smell within a few days. However, in Wells's view, the problem that human beings create is that their *ideas* about kinship do not match directly on to the facts of biological relatedness. '[W]e don't perform kin recognition in the way that animals do because we have the concept of kinship' (Wells, reported text of BAAS paper, Belfast).

Biological relatives, the speaker stated, are those with whom we share genes by descent. But we also 'recognize' other people as relatives who are not really relatives; aunt, she says, is often used to refer to people 'who are not really aunts'. The paper then went on to reveal the discovery that despite the kinds of concepts people hold about their kin, biologically related kin are often given preferential treatment. The author drew on a theory of kin selection that is much contested. None the less, these themes (kinship, relatedness, biology) were of enough moment to be reported at length in the quality press (*Guardian*, 28 August 1987).

As in other areas of scientific inquiry, discoveries in social science may follow the pattern of this one, bringing to light fresh facts about behaviour. But there are also those kinds of discovery that do not unearth fresh facts so much as make fresh connections. The present exercise falls into the second class. It explores some of the ways connections are made between facts, and does so in the light of an anthropological assumption about cultural practice.

The anthropological analysis of culture points to the general human facility for making ideas out of other ideas. We make fresh concepts by borrowing from one domain of life the imagery by which to structure other areas – as Darwin apparently did by finding in nineteenth-century ideas about degrees of kinship and affinity the vocabulary for his nascent theory of natural selection (Beer, 1983). But images pressed into new service acquire new meanings. Thus the idea of affinity between species gives fresh resonance to the idea of human affinity. Old meanings in turn are destabilized, and indeed the whole process may generate uncertainty. Hence the *Guardian* prints a story on kinship because changing practices in family relations mean we are not quite certain what to borrow or where to borrow from, the appropriate analogy to draw. Perhaps tadpoles and bees will help. But how we seek help already gives a shape to the problem.

Reproductive medicine is no exception. I suggest that the way in which changes in this field are conceptualized, and the way the choices that assisted reproduction affords are formulated, will affect thinking about kinship. And the way people think about kinship will affect other ideas about relatedness between human beings. What follows is a brief demonstration of connections between various aspects of kinship as they were aired at the time of the passing of the

Human Fertilization and Embryology Act, 1990. It pretends to analyse neither the parliamentary debates themselves nor the public debate as it was carried on in the press and in other publications, nor indeed does it presume that there is only one debate. Instead, it illustrates some common cultural strategies in the communication of concerns. The concerns address formulations about the nature of kinship that characterizes British society. Broadly, one may think of these formulations as 'Western' or Euro-American in so far as they are recognizable across Northern European and North American cultures; narrowly, one may think of them as belonging to specific forms of middle class consciousness and inquiry, of interest in this country in so far as they provide the language in whose terms evidence came before Parliament and was filtered back to the public via the press.

Robert Pritchard, a geneticist, recently complained about the way people are screened from scientific knowledge in reproductive medicine. Instead of being given the responsibility of making decisions for themselves, legislation makes it necessary for them to seek expert advice. Often this will be medical even though the issues surrounding the example he cites, surrogacy, are not medical but ethical and legal. What is interesting is that he borrowed an analogy from education: people learn, he is reported as saying (*Daily Telegraph*, 7 April 1990), through participation rather than formal instruction. This makes a connection for his observation that '[e]thical problems are problems for individuals, not legislation' (Pritchard, Meeting on Genetics and Society, University of Leicester). He thus used an assertion about learning to make an assertion about freedom of choice. It is exactly the manner in which he thus borrows one set of ideas (education) to talk about another (freedom) that enables me to make a counter-assertion. I shall also make connections, but of a different kind.

The statement about legislation seems to me misplaced. Ethical problems are problems for society, because – among other things – of the way they draw on and simultaneously challenge existing ideas about human life.

Biological relatives

Darwin drew on the prevailing ideas of his time concerning genealogy and relatedness between human beings in order to depict degrees of affinity between other species. In the twentieth century Euro-Americans have turned this back on itself, and conceive biological relatedness as primordial and prior to the constructs human beings build upon it. People even talk of biological relatives.

In ordinary parlance, a 'relative' means a kinsperson, that is, one whose degree of relationship is socially recognized. The whole point of Wells's paper was that non-human animals do not recognize kinship as we do. So to talk about siblings in other species is to repeat Darwin's loan: the idea of a relative is borrowed from the affairs of human beings. But we also see how this becomes a two-way traffic, since the idea of biology is borrowed in turn to depict an essential or intrinsic component of relatedness between human beings. Biological relatives, Wells claimed, are not only those who share genes but they are the 'real' relatives. Real relatives, her argument adds, are likely to exercise choice and preference on one another's behalf.

This two-way traffic of ideas makes the concept of kinship a hybrid of different elements. Human kinship is regarded as a fact of society rooted in facts of nature. Persons we recognize as kin divide into those related by blood or by marriage, that is, the outcome of or in prospect of procreation. However, the process of procreation as such is seen as belonging not to the domain of society but to the domain of nature. *Kinship thus connects the two domains.* This is a combination that Euro-Americans reproduce several times over in their ideas about relatedness between human beings, and it is such reproduction and repetitions that constitute cultural practice.

Let me give an example. Family life is held to be based on two separable but overlapping principles. On the one hand lies the social character of particular arrangements. Household composition, the extensiveness of kin networks, the conventions of marriage – these are socially variable. On the other hand lie the natural facts of life. Birth and procreation, the inheritance of genetic material, the developmental stages through which a child progresses – these are naturally immutable. To talk about 'kinship' is to refer to the manner in which the social arrangements are based on and provide the cultural context for the natural processes. Indeed, such an overlap of concepts supports the prevailing twentieth-century orthodoxy in much anthropological and other social science approaches to culture, namely that the subjects of study are 'social constructions'. In the case of kinship, what is at issue is the social construction of natural facts. At the same time, established critiques, including from anthropology, make it evident that what are taken as natural facts are themselves social constructions (see Franklin, 1990). What is revealed is another hybrid.

It is important to realize that this cultural practice – the way in which ideas from different domains are brought together – is not just the preserve of social scientists and their theories of social constructionism. It is endemic in Euro-American habits of thought. The Human Fertilization and Embryology Act, 1990 stipulates that a woman shall not be provided with treatment services unless account has been taken of the welfare of the child-to-be, including the child's need for a father. Now, as it was reported at the time (for example, *Guardian*, 21 June 1990), the need for a father was justified during the course of the House of Commons debate by reference to a domain of social fact that had nothing to do with relatedness and only tangentially bore on the child's development. The mover of the amendment in question was reported as arguing that we tinker at our peril 'with the concept of the family being a financial unit which needs two people'. He thus brought together two different domains of experience, establishing the focus of concern (here the family) by overlapping criteria. Families constitute relationships produced by procreation on the one hand and household or financial organization on the other.

The example shows something else. Connections are motivated. The importance of the father's presence is being justified by implicit reference to housekeeping and income support. The concept of the family as a financial unit thus grounds the argument about fathers. One could equally well imagine the reverse conceptual strategy: a reference to the desirability of maintaining children's relationships with their fathers grounding an argument about income support and taxation.

This kind of cross-referencing is so habitual that one hardly stops to think about it. But it plays a significant part in people's views of the world. What the speaker was grounding was a sense of reality. One set of ideas under dispute (whether or not the 'need' for a father should be part of treatment screening) is grounded in another set whose reality at that juncture is not questioned. At that juncture, the idea of the family as a financial unit needing two people is not under debate, precisely because it is being deployed as a taken-for-granted point of reference.

In the concept of biological relatives or in the idea of kinship as the social construction of natural facts, the biology and the natural facts are taken for granted. Euro-Americans do not ordinarily dispute what these are. Indeed, they may be colloquially unspecific.

Finch's investigations (1989) into patterns of family obligation in Britain came up time and again against the special place that people gave to 'blood' ties. The character of family life and kin connections is frequently grounded by reference to this domain of nature. The concept of a blood 'tie' symbolizes the further fact that relatives are seen to have a claim on one another by virtue of their physiological makeup. With respect to understandings in social science, Finch discusses competing theoretical claims over whether 'biology is at the centre of mutual support in families' (1989: 218), including kin selection theory (in this latter view, people are likely to favour their own 'because of the biological relationship between them'). But however disputed the theories, and whether one is thinking as a social scientist or not, everyone seems to take it for granted that *a biological relationship has significance for human affairs*.

The idea of a biological relationship does double symbolic service. As a taken-for-granted reference point, it is one way of grounding the distinctiveness of kin relations. But it itself also indicates what can be construed as immutable or taken for granted in the human condition, the natural facts of life that seem to lie prior to everything else.

An anthropologist would argue that to sustain a domain of ideas as a reference point is also to sustain its separateness. The 'difference' between domains is affirmed in their being brought into relation – as when one supplements the other. Hence reference to the family as a financial unit introduced a fresh dimension to the debate on parents. In the same way, to think of kinship as the social construction of natural facts at once combines and separates the domain of social affairs from the natural world. Neither dimension will entirely substitute for the other; both are necessary, and the difference between each sustained.

Individual kin roles within Euro-American kinship systems repeat this overlap. Each plays out the hybrid combination in microcosm. An unambiguous kinsperson is both related by blood *and* is one whose relationship is acknowledged in forms of intimate care. Schneider (1968) formalized this division for American kinship by talking of the distinction between substance and code for conduct. A mother both gives birth and nurtures her child; you share genes with your mother's sister, but she enters your life as an aunt because of the visits and presents. As a result, there may be a problem where the overlap does not completely hold, when one element but not the other seems present, as in the case of in-laws. I doubt whether our ancestors of (say)

200 years ago were troubled in quite the same manner. It is very much a post-Darwinian problem.

In twentieth-century culture, nature has increasingly come to mean biology (cf. Ingold, 1986). In turn this has meant that the idea of natural kinship had been biologized. What is to count as natural has acquired rather specific meanings. And one challenge that the new reproductive technologies hold is how they will affect these meanings in the future. Already they have introduced into regular parlance the distinction between 'social' and 'biological' parenthood. Now biological parenthood does not replicate with exactness the old concept of natural kinship. It reproduces the idea. But, in reproducing the idea, it also introduces a new difference.

There is a new ambiguity about what should count as natural. The 'natural' father was once the progenitor of a child born out of wedlock; the 'natural' mother was once the progenitor of a child relinquished for adoption. Ideally, the social parent combined both biological and legal credentials, though it was not ordinarily necessary to mark the parent in this way. Contemporary possibilities of artificial procreation introduce a new contrast between artificial and natural process: assisted reproduction creates the biological parent as a separate category. By the same process, the social parent becomes marked as potentially deficient in biological credentials. (Glover et al. (1989: 57)) refers to '*either* the social *or* the biological father' [my emphasis].) The effect is thus a displacement of earlier usages. So the 'natural' parent of the future, if one may extrapolate, may well turn out to be the one for whom no special techniques are involved and the one on whose behalf no special legislation is required. In that case it would be the natural parent who combined both biological and social/legal attributes.

In so far as kinship is thought of as combining social and natural domains, and is thus the place of overlap between them, the recognition of one component without the other always gives people pause. What is new is the assistance being given to each domain. The natural facts of procreation are being assisted by technological and medical advances. The social facts of kin recognition and relatedness are being assisted by legislation. Kinship is doubly assisted. There is a further outcome to such assistance, for it takes away the very concepts that made kinship itself a distinctive domain. There is little now to be taken for granted.

Assisting the making of persons

Treatments available for remedying 'impaired' fertility make explicit the widely shared cultural assumption that persons desire children of their own.

Now while the origin of genetic material has consequences for the person born of it, and is part of his or her identity, conception is held to depend neither on that identity nor on the relationship of the couple. It is thought to be a (natural) process that operates independently of human intention. Human intention gets no further than acting on the desire itself. I make the remark apropos Euro-American thinking on the matter and with certain very different kinship systems in mind. In Melanesia, for instance, much cultural effort can be expended on making sure that persons conceive in the right relational context: infertility may be attributed to deficiencies in social relations, and facilitation will then attend to people's intentions in the matter. By contrast, Euro-Americans find nothing exceptional in the possibility of facilitating the physical process, an operation regarded as independent of personal or social identity.

The paradoxical outcome is that facilitating the process does not automatically assist the making of parents. It assists the making of children, but then the English word 'child' means both offspring and young person. What is assisted is the making of persons, and specifically individual persons.

Debates concerning embryo experimentation reveal an interesting combination of ideas surrounding the creation of new human life. With whatever caution Parliament and the government's Committee of Inquiry had approached this topic (Warnock, 1985), there is no doubt many assumed that the 'central question of when a human being came into existence' (*Guardian*, 24 April 1990) was the issue. This entailed a further assumption. Life was seen to inhere in living cells, humanness in the fact that they are produced from human genetic material. But the point at which 'a human being' could be said to have emerged was presented as the point at which the *individuality* of the physical matter that will make up the future body and mind of a single entity could be discerned. With the establishment of the individual, in this view, comes a necessary condition for the establishment of the person, that is, an entity with potential moral claims on others. Yet those claims seem a consequence of, rather than a cause of, its personhood (and cf. Smart, 1987). No relationship with other persons, not even its parents, affects the way the issue of personhood is generally discussed.

There was considerable dispute as to what demarcates that individuality. It might be said to be a divine spark that sanctifies life from the 'beginning' of fertilization. It might be said that embryos at a developmental stage prior to brain formation and consciousness are not persons. The potential rather than actual consciousness of the embryo became an area of contest and controversy. However, whether people talked of a soul or of a mind, the presumption was that they were talking of a quality existing in the singular (for example, Ward, 1990: 110: 'a person is a subject of rational consciousness'). Yet, as Dyson remarks (1990: 99), as far as ethics are concerned one should also consider the possibility that the ethical unit cannot be the individual as such, for human beings exist only in interdependence with other human beings. This was not an issue that found easy formulation. It is interesting to consider why.

From one perspective, the answer is trivial: the parliamentary debate concerned embryos first, their status as a potential being was a secondary attribute; the legislation was not about defining persons. But, from another perspective, the absence fits certain general cultural suppositions that affect the way people think about kinship.

First, Euro-Americans tend to visualize interdependence in the abstract, and can imagine a person without reference to other persons. If the adult individual is dependent, he or she is dependent 'on society'. They do not use dependence on relatives to stand for interdependence in general (embeddedness in kin relations will not do as a symbol for membership in the wider society). Instead, they try to conceptualize interdependence through abstract and universal criteria such as common humanity or interaction between an organism and its environment. Dyson refers to an 'interdependent human community' rather than to the interdependence of specific persons.

Second, Euro-American ideas of individuality are grounded in notions of physical discreteness. Thus the House of Commons allegedly made up its mind about the admissibility of embryo experimentation by focusing on the '14-day limit'. Its significance was spelled out by reference to biological process: 14 days is just before the so-called primitive streak can be seen, the precursor of a specific and single embryo – 'the rubicon is crossed between molecular matter and a potential human being' (Morgan and Lee, 1991: 68). At the same time, two 'clearly defined populations of cells' are apparent, those that will form the embryo and those that will form the placental support system (1991: 68). The chair of the then Interim Licensing Authority is quoted as saying that the formation marks 'the beginning of a unique, human individual' (*Daily Telegraph*, 23 April 1990). At least, this was one of the forms in which biological information was conveyed to those debating the Bill.[1]

However controversial the particular limit, the *significance of individuality was not disputed*. The central question of when 'a human being' came into existence was answered unanimously: when one can recognize a unique individual.

At a yet later stage one might start to talk of a human personality or person. Indeed, if the issue of personhood had nothing to do with interpersonal relationships, it had everything to do with developmental stages. Now once an individual person is born, his or her needs and rights inevitably exist in relation to those of others, and the very necessity to legislate on such needs and rights comes from the fact that persons are never isolated from the actions, effects, presences of others. But in this dialogue conducted with respect to the being not yet born, the emergence of personhood itself was taken to be a natural process, the outcome of biological development rather than the person's own moral standing or participation in relationships with other persons.

So what becomes the issue at debate is the stage of growth. While other persons may act on behalf of the person-to-be as though it were already born, the embryo/fetus does not respond with a presence of its own. Or rather, its personhood is anticipated above all by reference to its physical presence. Of course action is taken on behalf of non-responsive entities all the time (Gallagher, 1987), as it is on behalf of persons with immature or impaired responsiveness. None the less, it is of some moment, I think, to imagine the very reproduction of persons in a non-relational way.

Like kinship, in the Euro-American view, individual persons are commonly construed as a hybrid of the two dimensions referred to earlier. On the one hand persons always inhabit a social and cultural world of which they are actively part and which they help to create; on the other hand they exist as naturally individual beings with needs and desires of their own. The dimensions overlap when the person is thought of as both a member of society and as an autonomous individual whose existence is defined by other criteria such as physiological and developmental processes. But there is also an asymmetry here. Indeed, the latter may be prioritized over the former: the one dimension (individuality) acts as a grounding and reference point for the other (personhood).

Assisting the making of parents

Discussions surrounding the prospects of 'assisted' reproduction make explicit the fact that no one comes into existence without the joining of complementary substances: one cannot exist without having parents.

It is an axiomatic tenet of Euro-American kinship reckoning that everyone has parents in this biological sense, whether or not one knows who they are. For the simple transmission of the substances themselves is thought to confer identity. Self-consciousness about identity in turn is interpreted as part of the individual's rights as a person: thus the child's 'right to know' the origin of its genetic makeup has been an important part of the debate ever since the Warnock Report (Warnock, 1985). But the interests of parents and children may conflict, and knowledge does not necessarily lead to relationship.

The child's right to know inevitably raises the question of its relationship to its 'biological parents'. It is from the consequences of such revelation (it was commonly argued) that those who donate reproductive material, but who do not wish to be known as parents, should be protected. In other words, what might be good for the child is not necessarily good for the parents. A different conflict emerges in the evaluation of parental involvement in the child's upbringing, for a further axiom of Euro-American kinship is that parents must give their children the right environment. Biological parenting and social parenting is thus combined again in the idea that the fitness of social parents turns on their ability to provide the proper natural circumstances for the child to grow up. The focus here is on the child's needs both as a developing organism and as an individual self with a psycho-emotional profile, so the parent becomes defined in relation to its perceived needs. It is assumed that these may compete with other aspects of the parents' lives as persons. Indeed, generally in Britain, the duties of parents to children are more clearly acknowledged than the duties of children to parents (see Finch, 1989). Inheritance aside, since duty and responsibility fall on the parent with respect to the child, it is assumed that parenthood should be recognized in law. But the law finds itself acknowledging biological parenthood even where one might have thought its business was the definition of social parenthood.

A distinction between social and legal recognition is traditional. The former concerned the acknowledgement of a relationship, the latter rights in law. Thus the Glover Report can consider the case of Swedish law, where the semen donor is socially recognized in that the child at age 18 has a right to know who he is, but he has no rights of legal paternity in the child. The implication is that it is desirable to match legal paternity to social rather than biological paternity as far as the family in which the child will grow up is concerned. 'Social parenthood often out-ranks biological parenthood . . . And the emotional bond with the social father is usually far more important to children than the genetic links with the donor' (Glover et al., 1989: 35). The social relationship, however, is still being justified in reference to a biological process of sorts, the process being a universal one concerning the child's needs as a developing human being. So while a social parent is given preference over a biological parent, the significance of the social parent is once again established by reference to a non-social aspect of development. In this imagery, 'the relationship' does not exist between persons, then, so much as between the mutuality of their natural needs.

Debates over who shall be regarded by society as parents, then, are *not* the mirror image of debates over the beginning of life, and that is because of the priority that the biological facts of life have in grounding the very perception of the 'real' situation. Hence the same asymmetry to which I referred. Thus the discussion over human beginnings proceeds without reference to social factors at all: when a person begins is taken as a biological fact of individual development. By contrast, the legal debate over who shall be socially acknowledged as parent makes constant reference to biological parenting: legislation is after the fact.

The reason for this asymmetry rests in the two points already made. First, it is possible to conceive of a child as having claims on society directly and in its own right. Its relationship with its parents is enabling for personal development, but its claims as a full moral and legal individual are on society in general rather than on its parents in particular. Parents only mediate this future relationship and, if necessary, society in the form of the state can intervene to protect the child's welfare. Second, the individuality of persons is imagined in terms of their uniqueness (physical discreteness) as functioning organisms. A person's social life is regarded as extrinsic: in interactions with others the individual person is influenced or affected by them, but such interdependence frequently appears negotiable. People become parents because parents are said to want children of 'their own'. The colloquialism, an interesting fusion of whom one identifies with and what one owns against the world, points to desire or preference. The child has no choice as to which parents are its own, but may prefer to escape their influence or spurn their property: it is the person's individual status not its relationships which guarantee its own personhood.

As a result, attempts to define relationships, such as that between parent and child, render the actual notion of relationship elusive. On the one hand, Euro-Americans make the maintenance of relationships dependent on the preference of persons (for example, 'in the end ethical decisions are made by taking into account human preference', Ward, 1990: 112), which echoes the remark quoted at the beginning of this chapter (the idea that ethical problems are problems for individuals). Persons, as we have seen, are thought of as individual subjects. On the other hand, in so far as social arrangements are regarded as constructions on natural facts, themselves perceived as above all biological facts, people feel that definitions of relationship should incorporate and pay attention to these facts. Social relationships appear contingent. These points connect two versions of the same construct. Biology is rooted in an order of reality to which social arrangements must attend, not the other way round.

We are used to this asymmetry in the definitions of 'mother' and 'father'. The two are not mirror images of each other either. The division between what we now see as biological and social parents, or between the biological and social identities of any single parent, is also reproduced in the division between the evidently biological involvement of the mother with her child and the necessity to presume and therefore socially construct fatherhood. Even where what is at issue is the father's biological contribution, that is popularly supposed to depend on social acknowledgement in a way a mother's parenthood is not.

Sections 27 and 28 of the British Human Fertilization and Embryology Act determine the 'meaning of "mother"' and the 'meaning of "father"' in certain cases of assisted conception. The woman who is the carrier of the child is in law to be treated as the mother. The explanatory notes to the Bill added, 'whether or not the child is genetically hers'. As far as the father is concerned, the Act provides for the husband of a married woman who has conceived through donation to be treated in law as the father of the child so long as he consented to the donation. This follows the recommendation of the Warnock Report, in relation to which Rivière (1985) pointed out some time ago that the intention to treat a person *as* a mother or father implies that this is a social construction (a legal 'fiction') on the natural facts. In this case, the natural fact is that he is not the biological (genetic) father. Commentators (Morgan and

Lee, 1991: 154–6) interpret the protection of anonymity afforded sperm donors as, in the absence of any consent from a husband or other man, creating the legally 'fatherless' child. It is not that a real father (the genetic father) does not exist, but (as they see it) that the law forbids his being socially acknowledged.

In the past, the natural facts that define a mother always seemed more comprehensive than those defining her partner. She both donated genetic material and brought the child to term, elements combined in the former cultural assumption that childbirth was a supreme natural fact of life. Now the period of gestation has become culturally ambiguous, and in the new division between biological and social motherhood, the mother's nurturing role shifts from being regarded as part of a total biological process to being the principal attribute of a social one. At the same time, the very conceptualization of artificial or assisted conception means that the pre-birth process is no longer a definitive natural fact either.

In Western (Euro-American) middle class culture, parenthood traditionally presumed a relationship between persons. Yet there was a constant lopsidedness or asymmetry to the depiction of relationships for the very reason that they appeared to be constructed after natural facts. The converse was the supposition that if there is a biological tie, then there is always the question of whether or not social recognition should follow. Yet current legislative attempts to define who shall be the parent when faced with a range of choices, introduces an explicitness that may make the *fact* of relationship more rather than less uncertain. Being donor of reproductive resources, provider of gestatory facilities, postnatal nurturer – as separate elements none is sufficient grounds for acknowledging the connection as a relationship. A decision has to be taken on what kind of social relation is desirable as a consequence of the biological one.

In making a new convention, the distinction between social and biological parenting, out of an old one, kinship as the social construction of natural facts, the new reproductive technologies have provided unprecedented alternatives for legislation. Legislation in turn creates new explicitness. The Glover Report, a document suffused with an ideology of preference and choice, is hopeful that 'our ability to separate social from biological parenthood may create new patterns of relationship' (Glover et al., 1989: 53). I suggest three outcomes over which we may have little cultural choice.

First, the chances are that we shall go on trying to accommodate the representation of relationships to what is perceived as their natural basis – whether in biology at large or in genetics. The justifications and representations will change as fast as our views of the facts change. Given the determining role we accord to the biology, how we represent those facts to ourselves will thus affect us all.

Second, while social relationships appear to respond to and deal with biological facts, from an anthropologist's point of view those facts are also cultural facts, constructs that are themselves socially or culturally motivated. We are in something of a new area when they become legally motivated. Which points of law are going to apply to the management of the natural world can be expected to play an increasingly significant part in our lives. Even being able to conceive of life forms as subject to patent, for instance, offers intriguing analogies for the proprietorship of persons.

Finally, the rooting of social relations in natural facts traditionally served to impart a certain quality to one significant dimension of kin relations. For all that one exercised choice, it was also the case that these relations were at base non-negotiable. The idea of a blood tie symbolized their given nature. There was a matter-of-factness to them that did not just concern the performance of kin obligations, important as that was. Ties of kinship in general stood for what was immutable about one's social circumstances by contrast with what was open to change. In being urged these days always to exercise preference and choice, we may find ourselves acting out a curious version of those kin selection theories to which Wells briefly referred (see above), and which themselves incorporated a version of Euro-American kinship thinking. Selecting which relatives one chooses to keep up with is one thing; selecting one's parentage is another.

The fatherless child

This brings me back to the manner in which we assist ourselves. In effect, Euro-Americans are being forced to be explicit about aspects of their own social and cultural practices in attempting to meet the needs they perceive.

In the same year as Wells's address, a short article appeared in the journal *Free Associations* on 'The crisis of fatherhood'. Its questioning of the notion of fatherhood is modelled by way of analogy on that of motherhood: 'Who is the father? Is he the man who provides the sperm . . . or the man who cares for the child?' (Smith, 1987: 72). The choice of the word 'care' rather than 'provide' was apparently deliberate, for the author attempts to put (social) fathering on the same nurturant footing as mothering. What prompts Smith's question is the issue of artificial insemination. It is not that assisted procreation is new, then, but that it has entered the cultural repertoire in such a way as to make such questions relevant to *any* conceptualization of parenthood.

Not surprisingly, Smith finds that fathers and mothers are not mirror images of each other. In asking about the emotional weight men put on biological fatherhood he discovers that their physical involvement cannot match women's: 'I as a man have not become pregnant, nor borne a child, nor am I breast-feeding one with my body milk. Unlike a woman, I am not *physically* tied to any one child once conception occurs' (1987: 75, emphasis in original).

The implication seems to be that emotional bonds flow from physical ones. As a result, doubts (his term) can be expressed at every stage, for at every stage there are new doubts about the physical ties. There are doubts about the relevance of male sexuality to conception, about the fact of genetic fatherhood, about the desirability of cohabitation, how one manages emotional dependency and the practicalities of child care and male labour. Doubts about the physical ties are doubts about relationships. In essence, this self-analysis takes apart an already established combination of social and natural relations. Break the parental role down into its components, and at no point does there seem an essential connection between the physical person and the social relationship of parent to child. Smith suggests this is particularly true of men. Women, not men, tend to take responsibility for contraception, he says; women are more certain than men of their biological parenting; women seem able to dispense with cohabitation as a precondition for bringing up a child, and so forth. But the comparisons he makes are merely one instance of a whole series of cultural connections between what is certain and what is uncertain in kinship arrangements, a version of the connection repeated over and again between natural-biological and social-legal parenthood.

The doubts remain real, and point in one direction. Unless a relationship is grounded in some intrinsic or natural connection, then Euro-Americans are likely to think of it as artificial and to be thought artificial is to be open to uncertainty. Reality must lie elsewhere.

The new reproductive technologies and the legislative and other actions to which they have given rise seek to assist natural process on the one hand and the social definition of kinship on the other. But this double assistance creates new uncertainties. For the present cultural explicitness is revolutionizing former combinations of ideas and concepts. The more we give legal certainty to social parenthood, the more we cut from under our feet assumptions about the intrinsic nature of relationships themselves. The more facilitation is given to the biological reproduction of human persons, the harder it is to think of a domain of natural facts independent of social intervention.

Whether or not all this is a good thing is uncertain. What is certain is that it will not be without consequence for the way people think about one another.

Notes

In addition to stimulus from Sarah Franklin and Frances Price, I must thank Erica Haimes for her careful reading of this chapter and many elucidating comments.

1 Because knowledge in this field is advancing at such a fast rate, the information that came to the House was not only translated for a lay audience but inevitably contained already out-of-date formulations that in turn 'mixed' with formulations already held (e.g. the idea that fertilization could be said to have a beginning).

References

Beer, Gillian (1983) *Darwin's Plots. Evolutionary Narrative in Darwin, George Eliot and Nineteenth Century Fiction.* London: Routledge and Kegan Paul.

Dyson, Anthony (1990) 'At Heaven's command? The churches, theology and experiments on embryos', in A. Dyson and J. Harris (eds), *Experiments on Embryos.* London: Routledge.

Finch, Janet (1989) *Family Obligations and Social Change.* Cambridge: Polity Press.

Franklin, Sarah (1990) 'Deconstructing "desperateness": the social construction of infertility in popular representations of new reproductive technologies', in M. McNeil, I. Varcoe and S. Yearley (eds), *The New Reproductive Technologies.* Basingstoke: Macmillan.

Gallagher, Janet (1987) 'Eggs, embryos and foetuses: anxiety and the law', in M. Stanworth (ed.), *Reproductive Technologies.* Cambridge: Polity Press.

Glover, Jonathan and others (1989) *Fertility and the Family.* The Glover Report on Reproductive Technologies to the European Commission. London: Fourth Estate.

Ingold, Tim (1986) *Evolution and Social Life*. Cambridge: Cambridge University Press.

Morgan, Derek and Lee, Robert (1991) *Blackstone's Guide to the Human Fertilization and Embryology Act, 1990: Abortion and Embryo Research, the Law*. London: Blackstone Press.

Rivière, Peter (1985) 'Unscrambling parenthood: the Warnock Report', *Anthropology Today*, 4: 2–7.

Schneider, David M. (1968) *American Kinship: A Cultural Account*. Englewood Cliffs, NJ: Prentice-Hall.

Smart, Carol (1987) ' "There is of course the distinction created by nature": law and the problem of paternity', in M. Stanworth (ed.), *Reproductive Technologies*. Cambridge: Polity Press.

Smith, Gavin (1987) 'The crisis of fatherhood', *Free Associations*, 9: 72–90.

Ward, Keith (1990) 'An irresolvable dispute?', in A. Dyson and J. Harris (eds), *Experiments on Embryos*. London: Routledge.

Warnock, Mary (1985) *A Question of Life: The Warnock Report on Human Fertilization and Embryology*. Oxford: Basil Blackwell.

8
Conclusion

Our aim in writing this book based on papers from the 1990 Sociology Section of the British Association for the Advancement of Science annual conference was to make available to a wider audience a social science perspective on new reproductive techniques such as *in vitro* fertilization, semen and egg donation. It is our belief that this perspective could be helpful to individuals, professionals and policy makers in coming to terms with the changes and the problems they are facing in consequence of the introduction of these techniques. We think the evidence of the preceding chapters has begun to demonstrate the many social and cultural connections of assisted reproduction which the social sciences can bring to light. The evidence has also indicated the many levels which are revealed in analysing these connections: the conceptual, the cultural, the political and the practical.

When there are problems to face it is helpful to understand what is new and what is old in their constitution. Naomi Pfeffer's historical review in Chapter 3 did just that for the infertility services, revealing the involvement of both conceptual and political levels. In political terms many interests have been involved. Successive British governments have taken little action over issues to do with reproduction, not only because of the libertarian traditions of the country, but also because of the conflicting interest groups in the electorate. This partly explains continued government avoidance of an overt population policy and also of any close involvement in reproductive issues. Futhermore, while human reproduction can be, and often is, conceptualized as a matter of population policy, British governments have defined it as a health issue, but have not given it a high priority in the health service. So infertility services, including the delivery of the new and expensive procedures of assisted reproduction, have been left largely to the private sector. In this context government initiative in the 1990 Human Fertilization and Embryology Act represented a new departure. The main focus was not on infertility, however, but on gametes and embryos. The implications for the children of assisted reproduction and their various parents were examined and finally regulated from this largely biological standpoint.

Where Naomi Pfeffer focused on historical continuities in the reproductive story, Sarah Franklin in Chapter 4 pointed to the changes already made and currently taking place in the way conception is thought about. At one level her chapter gives us some insight into the practical problems faced by the women who are the 'reproductive pioneers' undergoing IVF. They become technically quite expert in the procedures but nevertheless have difficulty understanding the meaning for themselves of what is happening to them; they also have problems in communicating to others about their experiences.

At another level Sarah Franklin's research shows how, in changing the narrative about conception, the procedures introduced to override infertility are also changing the culture of our society. In British culture, and in Euro-American culture more generally, conception has been seen as a set of 'natural facts' and has been told as a story about how babies are conceived, involving the journey of the sperm to meet and fertilize the egg. However, in the world of achieved conception, this story is becoming more complex, less certain, less 'natural' and, paradoxically, more mysterious the more the biological processes are opened to scientific gaze.

As the 'natural facts' change so do the social facts and the cultural meanings, for as Sarah Franklin has shown the conception stories are cultural cosmologies in microcosm. They celebrate the values of our kind of society, values to do with industrialism, technology, scientific progress, the control of nature for the betterment of humankind; they celebrate also the great social institutions of medicine, law, commerce and the state. But the conception stories are also relevant to each of us at the personal level, defining as they do identity, relationships and kinship obligations. Here the relevance of the culture to the problems of daily living become very clear.

Other practical problems may ensue from assisted reproduction, as Frances Price made plain in Chapter 5. The great majority of women undergoing procedures such as IVF or GIFT will not achieve their long-desired goal of giving birth to a live baby, as the data on the IVF record presented in Chapter 2 demonstrates. For those who find themselves with three or more babies to care for, the problems are of a different kind. They are about how to feed, clothe, mind, train and teach so many same-age children at once with the resources – human, social and economic – which are ordinarily available for one child at a time. Frances Price's account makes it clear that in making arrangements to overcome the biological problem of infertility, little thought was given to the social and emotional aspects of possibly having so many children at once. Such an event renders the familiar unfamiliar and the normal abnormal.

Higher order births occurring before assisted reproduction was introduced were rare and called forth exceptional responses: there were no routine ways to handle them. Nowadays higher order births resulting from medical intervention, while not an everyday occurrence, are sufficiently common no longer to attract exceptional responses. Yet no appropriate routine arrangements to provide adequate services and resources have been made, for such events are nevertheless 'not normal', nor are they planned for on an individual basis. Much human suffering is consequently involved.

There is a disjunction here between, on the one hand, the elaborate and expensive procedures applied to try to achieve conception and subsequent birth and, on the other, the failure of social understanding about the consequences for the human beings involved if the procedures miscarry or over-succeed, if one may so describe the eventuality of higher order births. This disjunction seems to arise from a capacity in our culture to think of the biological on its own without reference to the social. This theme has emerged throughout this book, but particularly clearly in the chapters by Erica Haimes and Marilyn Strathern.

In Chapter 6 Erica Haimes showed that in the two sides of the argument about whether semen or egg donors should or should not be anonymous, part of the common ground which both share is the importance of genetic ties: no one among the Warnock committee members she interviewed or in the literature she reviewed suggested that genetic origins were of no consequence. No one, that is, argued the case that a child is a child is a person in her or his own right and as he or she is, to be accepted as such no matter what his or her genetic origins, who carried her or him to term or nourished him or her.

There are other cultural commonalities between the opposed sides in the anonymity argument. The importance of the historical past again emerges. Anonymity had been insisted on in the early days of donor insemination. All protagonists now start from this standpoint. It is, however, possible to conceptualize the problem differently and start by asking the question why, simply because of their different mode of conception, these people are treated differently from others?

At a practical level Erica Haimes suggested that one way of resolving the anonymity debate, having recognized the common ground, might be through the language of rights, for that discourse cannot avoid squarely addressing the social. Theoretically she advised that establishing a range of family forms rather than defending particular types of family relationships and family units may be a fruitful way forward. Empirically, after all, a wide range of family forms exist: the increasing number of children who are stepchildren in the house of one or other parent and move between each, for example.

Marilyn Strathern in the penultimate chapter has helped to identify a crucial piece of conceptualization which goes far to explain the anomalies Erica Haimes's research uncovered. This crucial element is the asymmetry in the way Euro-Americans think about the relationship between the 'natural' or 'biological' and the social in human reproduction: the biological is always assumed to be involved, but not necessarily the social. So she finds that, in discussions of when an embryo may be said to be human and have the potential for individuality, the references made are entirely to biological aspects of the conceptus. Lawyers when discussing the rights of the fetus or of the subsequent child do make reference to the social, but they always *also* refer to the biological. Indeed genetic origins may be felt to be crucial to identity. Couples' wish to have 'a child of their own' is strong, as witness the numbers prepared to go through IVF procedures. There is concern that children and adults should be able to know, if they so wish, who their 'real' parents are or what were their genetic origins in cases where responsibility for parenthood is shared among a number of people, as may now be the case.

Together these papers help to elucidate some of the reasons for the initial failure – about which Meg Stacey complained in Chapter 2 – of official inquiries, funding bodies and others to recognize that the social sciences have a distinctive contribution to add to the clinical, the ethical and the legal. For our researches have shown that the assumption from which Meg Stacey started her comments, namely that birth is as much a social event as it is a biological one, is not commonly shared in our culture. There are many who only perceive the biological and thus make biological interventions without any detailed thought for their social consequences either for the individuals involved or for the society at large.

Our claim is different. Interventions in the biological may have beneficent or malevolent consequences for those who experience them, but social and cultural consequences there certainly will be. These consequences will spread far beyond the relatively small numbers of women who now undergo the procedures. This will happen partly because assisted reproduction will be used in an increasing number of obstetric interventions aimed to remove or modify genetic defects. It is also because the medical interventions, which have become increasingly sophisticated and complex over the past 200 years, constitute, in Meg Stacey's words, a scientific revolution. This has already profoundly changed the way we think about birth and the responsibilities involved in it and is now changing the way we think about conception. Not only those experiencing the interventions are being affected, but all of us. A new culture and structure for our society is being created along with the changes in human reproduction.

A matter of such importance deserves much more research attention than it has hitherto received. For example, in decisions about how to regulate the new techniques and how to use them much reliance is placed on certain long-standing cultural characteristics and ways of looking at the world. Yet those very cultural characteristics are changing, in large part *directly* because of the introduction of the new techniques themselves, although other social and cultural events and processes are also at work. To base new models of use and control upon a model which is ceasing to exist is bound to introduce difficulties for the future.

We have referred a good deal in the preceding chapters to a generalized Euro-American culture, which we have argued has had particular consequences for the application and regulation of the new techniques. Yet we have also noted in passing that there are cross-cultural and cross-national differences. The use of bodies or body parts as commodities, for example, is handled differently in the United States and the UK, the latter country having made the buying and selling of parts or the renting of wombs illegal. The German refusal to permit embryo research because of that country's uncomfortable memories of the abuse of genetics during the Nazi era is a stark and obvious example of the effect of social and cultural differences.

In these chapters we have only been able to allude to a few such matters. Our central thesis of the importance of the social and cultural in the applications of the new reproductive techniques indicates that there is a strong case for systematic comparative examination of these international differences. Such research would help to reveal variations in what is seen as 'natural', what interventions may be accepted as tolerable and what as intolerable. We anticipate from the comparative evidence already available that the research would underline our claim that birth is as much a social as a biological event, the handling of which is crucially affected by cultural characteristics.

Meg Stacey referred to the frequent use in debate and discussion of the notion of the 'slippery slope' down which the new techniques and their control mechanisms may cause our society to slide. If we are able to see that human reproduction – assisted or 'natural' – is itself essentially a *social* act, we shall the better be able to see the alternative paths we could choose to tread, rather than feeling we are the victims of uncontrollable forces. Such understanding might lead, for example, to a recognition that controls need to come at rather different points than they do at present; that, for example, medical procedures such as IVF or GIFT should not have been established without proper analyses being undertaken of their likely social consequences. Now they are with us, it seems crucial that their social and cultural consequences should be continually monitored.

Much further research is needed to demonstrate the ways

in which connections between the biological, social and cultural arise and are sustained. In such a fundamental (and as we now learn, complex) matter as human reproduction the labours of many disciplines are and will be needed to analyse and assess the issues. Lawyers and ethicists are already heavily involved: we hope the evidence presented here will have shown that the social sciences also have a distinctive and vital contribution to make.

Glossary

CMAC/SA FPA Contemporary Medical Archives: Family Planning Association.

CMAC/SA EUG Contemporary Medical Archives: Eugenics Society.

Conceptus The product of the union of sperm and ovum; sometimes used to avoid the problems around the definition of embryo (q.v.).

DHSS Department of Health and Social Security; established in 1968 by amalgamation of the former Ministry of Health (q.v.) and the Ministry of National Insurance (q.v.).

DOH, D of H or **DH** Department of Health; established in 1988 by the splitting of DHSS (q.v.) into a Department of Health and a Department of Social Security (DSS; q.v.).

DNA Deoxyribonucleic acid: the type of molecule of which genes are made and which carries the coded information specifying the precise chemistry of an organism, including humans, and its pattern of development; DNA is composed of two long strands wound as in a double helix.

DSS Department of Social Security; established in 1988 to administer unemployment, sickness and old age benefits.

EACHR European Advisory Committee for Health Research: a committee of the European Region of the World Health Organization whose task it is to advise the European Region about priorities in health research which it should recommend to member states.

Embryo Definitions vary; formerly used to describe the first 6–8 weeks from fertilization of the ovum, after which time the embryo is said to be recognizably human and is then called the fetus (q.v.). Some now refer to the first 14 days from the meeting of sperm and egg as a pre-embryo and use embryo for the end of that period to the time when it is called a fetus. In the UK the Human Fertilization and Embryology Act defined embryo as an egg in the process of fertilization.

ESRC Economic and Social Research Council: an independent government-funded body which in the UK allocates state funds for research in the social sciences.

Fetus Formerly usually spelled foetus in the UK; the unborn infant which has developed from the embryo (q.v.) to a stage where it is said to be recognizably human, i.e. after about eight weeks gestation.

FINRRAGE Feminist International Network for Resistance to Reproductive and Genetic Engineering: a pressure group whose name describes its purpose.

FPA Family Planning Association: a voluntary body which in the UK offered contraceptive and infertility advice.

FSH Follicle-stimulating hormone (see gonadotrophins).

Gamete A sex-cell, either ovum (female) or sperm (male).

Gestation The term used to describe a pregnancy, especially relating to its duration, normally about 38 weeks.

GIFT Gamete (q.v.) intrafallopian transfer: eggs and sperm are mixed in the laboratory and immediately replaced in the woman's tubes so that fertilization occurs inside her body.

Gonadotrophins Sometimes spelled gonadotropins; hormones produced by the anterior lobe of the pituitary gland (called the 'master gland' because it governs the processes of reproduction). The follicle-stimulating hormone (FSH) stimulates the maturation of the follicles in the ovaries in which eggs are developed. Luteinising hormone (LH) initiates ovulation. Both hormones are present throughout the menstrual cycle; FSH predominates in the pre-ovulatory phase while the level of LH surges just before ovulation. The way in which both hormones influence fertility is incompletely understood. Gonadotrophins (which are proteins) administered to infertile women are effective only if extracted from raw materials (blood and urine) provided by other women. Powerful drugs, they elicit an unpredictable response; risks attached are hyperstimulation of the woman's ovaries with occasionally serious consequences; multiple ovulation, multiple conception, multiple births.

HFEA Human Fertilization and Embryology Authority: the statutory body set up in the UK under the 1990 Human Fertilization and Embryology Act to succeed the ILA (q.v.) in the regulation of embryo research and infertility treatment centres, including licensing and inspection.

ILA Interim Licensing Authority for Human *In Vitro* Fertilization and Embryology: the name taken by the VLA (q.v.) in 1989 to underline their view that a statutory body was needed.

IVF *In vitro* fertilization: eggs and sperm are mixed and fertilized in the laboratory, i.e. outside the body; the resultant conceptus (q.v.) is then inserted in the woman's womb.

LH Luteinising hormone (see gonadotrophins).

Ministry of Health. Established in 1919 to administer the medical element of the national insurance (q.v.) scheme; after 1948 it administered the NHS.

Ministry of National Insurance. Administered the sickness and unemployment benefits provided under the national insurance (q.v.) scheme.

MRC Medical Research Council: an independent government-funded body which in the UK allocates state funds for research in medicine.

National Insurance. Established in 1911 to provide social and medical insurance to significant sections of the working population.

NHS National Health Service: the nation-wide, mainly state-funded, British health care provision originally free at the point of delivery which came into existence in July 1948.

NPEU National Perinatal Epidemiology Unit: a research unit in Oxford, England, working on issues around childbirth and early infancy.

OPCS Office of Population Censuses and Surveys: a UK government office whose name describes its function.

PRO Public Records Office, where UK public records are lodged.

RCOG Royal College of Obstetricians and Gynaecologists; the body responsible in the UK for the specialties of obstetrics and gynaecology.

VLA Voluntary Licensing Authority for Human *In Vitro* Fertilization and Embryology: the body set up voluntarily in the UK by the RCOG (q.v.) and the MRC (q.v.) to regulate the use of procedures such as IVF (q.v.) and associated research.

Warnock Committee The committee established in 1982 to advise government on human fertilization and embryo research and to advise on its regulation as necessary. The committee's report was published by DHSS/HMSO in 1984 as Cm. 9314. In the subsequent year it was republished by Basil Blackwell under Mary Warnock's name as *A Question of Life* with a further introduction and conclusion written by her.

WHO World Health Organization.

WHO EURO The European Region of the World Health Organization.

Index

2363